AF321564

FRANCES HODGKINS

This book is from a series about Modern Women Artists
published by Eiderdown Books.

Other titles available from the same series:

01 *Sylvia Pankhurst*
by Katy Norris

02 *Frances Hodgkins*
by Samantha Niederman

03 *Marlow Moss*
by Lucy Howarth

04 *Laura Knight*
by Alice Strickland

05 *Lee Miller*
by Ami Bouhassane

To order books, please visit eiderdownbooks.com

FRANCES HODGKINS

Samantha Niederman

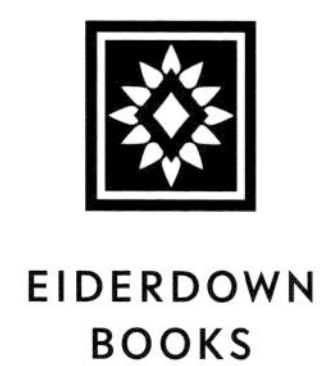

EIDERDOWN
BOOKS

MODERN WOMEN ARTISTS

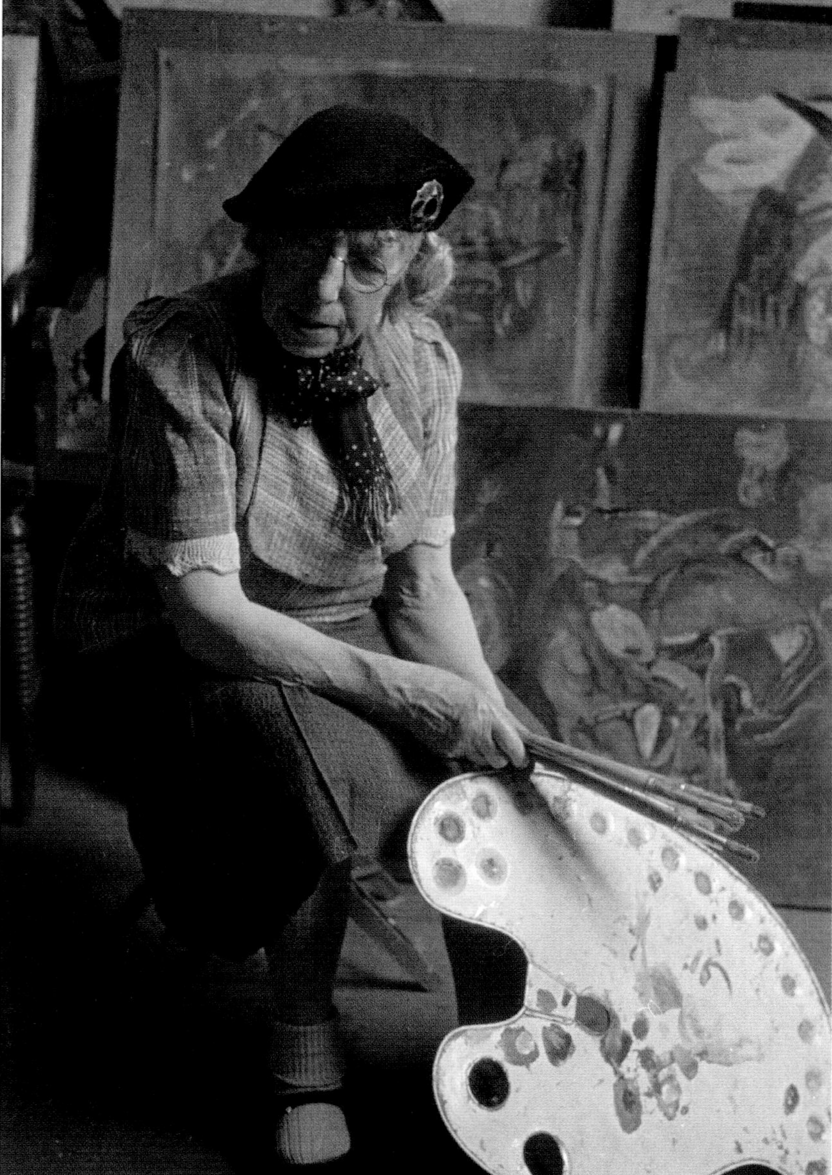

Born in Dunedin, the South Island of New Zealand, Frances Hodgkins (1869–1947) was a groundbreaking modern artist (Fig. 1). For the first 30 years of her life, Hodgkins trained and worked as a colonial Impressionist, but she yearned for more, and sought to 'measure [herself] against the moderns'.[1] At the turn of the century, Hodgkins was the first female painter of her generation to leave her successful nineteenth-century career back home in New Zealand in order to advance her artistic training in Europe. While in Paris, direct contact with modern art transformed Hodgkins' own work and resulted in her recognition at the centre of the art world at this time. Hodgkins, who did not believe that being a woman was any kind of limitation, continued to cultivate a professional reputation, which lead to her appointment as the first woman artist to teach at the *Académie Colarossi* in Paris in 1910. In Britain throughout the 1930s and 1940s, Hodgkins' original art and pioneering principles resulted in her inclusion as the only woman amongst 18 artists to be featured in *The Penguin Modern Painters* series. This distinction cemented Hodgkins' position as the first internationally recognised female Modernist at the forefront of the British avant-garde.

1. Frances Hodgkins at her studio in Corfe Castle village, Dorset, 1945

Trailblazing Transitions: From Colonial Impressionist to International Modernist

By 1895, Hodgkins was determined to travel abroad to further her education and to develop her painting in response to European modern art. The majority of professional artists in New Zealand at this time were men, while female artists were mainly acknowledged as amateurs, who painted for a hobby alongside their primary responsibilities of homemaking and child-rearing. Rejecting these traditional roles, Hodgkins wrote: 'I have only one prominent idea and that is that nothing will interfere between me and my work.'[2] Indeed, by the end of her life in 1947, Hodgkins' artistic identity had evolved from a colonial Impressionist into an experimental avant-gardist, who had conquered twentieth-century British Modernism. But what is the significance of this momentous shift in the development of her style and technique? From the nineteenth to the first half of the twentieth century, New Zealand painters essentially identified as transposed British artists and as such, appropriated a continental taste for the great practitioners of classical landscapes such as Nicolas Poussin and Claude Lorrain. Hodgkins resisted this conservative fascination with creating idealised, picturesque and unrealistic New Zealand landscapes. In fact, even in her earliest works, she avoided landscapes entirely. Instead, she focused on portraiture and figure studies, which evoke the sentimentality of Victorian painting, but also indicate independence in her choice of genres.

The earliest turning point in Hodgkins' career as a Modernist can be traced to the first of her three separate voyages to Europe made in 1901. During this first journey, Hodgkins continued to paint similar motifs to those from her initial period – sensitive figure studies and portraits in watercolour – but her immediate introduction to more avant-garde art, especially in Paris, transformed her techniques and subject matter. Works such as *Calves for Sale, Les Andelys, Normandy*

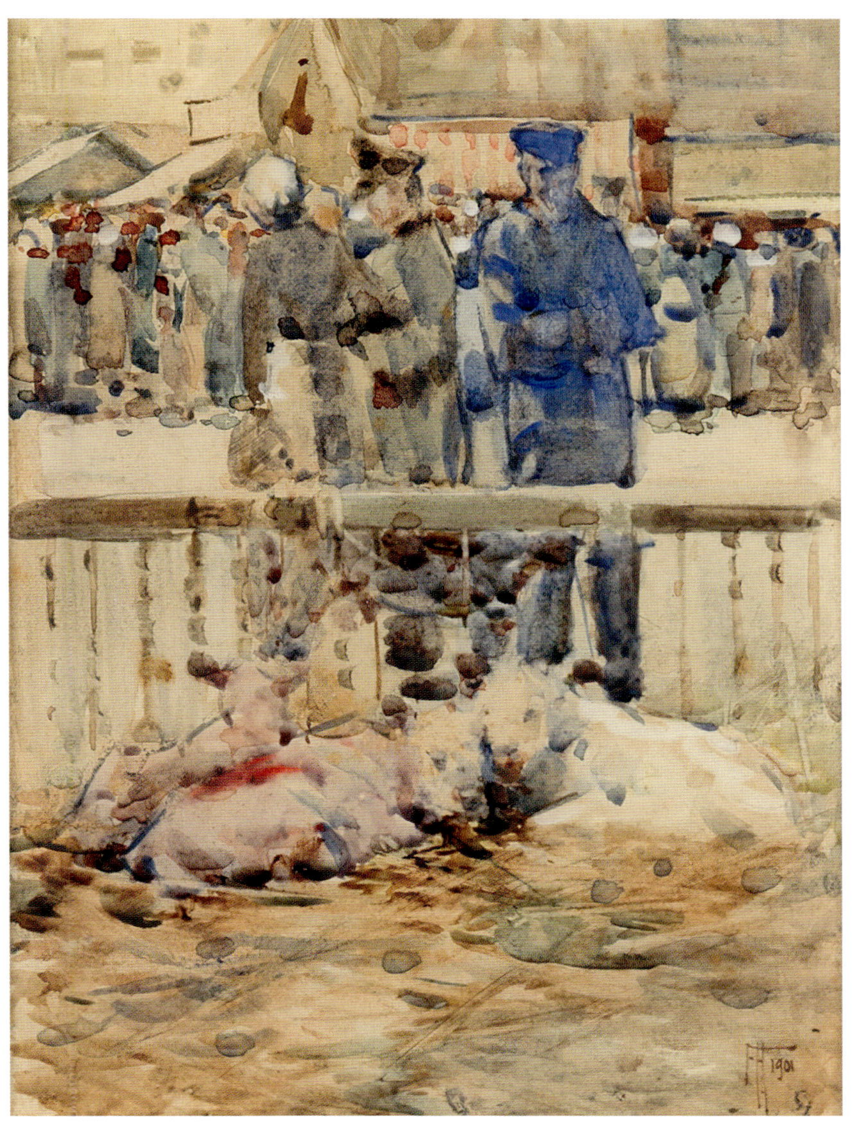

2. *Calves for Sale, Les Andelys, Normandy*, 1901, watercolour

(Fig. 2) demonstrate Hodgkins' early engagement with Modernism through her use of a wet-on-wet method, which enabled her to distil the bustling market scene, enhancing its patchwork of colours with Impressionistic dabs of paint. Of the farmer in the foreground examining the calves, Hodgkins wrote: '... some of the old men wear such beautiful blue corduroy bags that make me ache to paint them ...'[3] Hodgkins' employment of subjective individuality through her daring use of the colour blue links her art with that of the Symbolists and the Fauvists such as Odilon Redon and Henri Matisse; artists who composed paintings with visionary colours and abstracted forms to elicit the expression of inner sensations. Rather than painting literal descriptions, Hodgkins also began to convey the motif's inner spirit, which quickly distinguished her from her New Zealand contemporaries.

Less than three years after her arrival in Europe, Hodgkins became the first New Zealand-born artist to have one of her watercolours exhibited at the Royal Academy of Arts in London (RA) – one of the highest honours for painters in Britain; her art would continue to be selected for the Academy's exhibitions over subsequent years. Despite her early success in Britain, Hodgkins continued to travel to exotic destinations in order to find fresh inspiration for her work. Tangier, Morocco, a place where few female artists dared to go at this time, was where Hodgkins painted The Orange Sellers, Tangier (Fig. 3). Although the subject of this watercolour is another market scene, the lower half of the composition – a loosely modelled display of colourful produce – is Hodgkins' main focus, prefiguring her fascination with, and transformation of, the still life genre itself. Of the vibrant mass of colours, the artist wrote: 'it is the apple or rather the onion of my eye ... a jumble of onions melons & oranges ... I am going to eschew vegetables after this with a comfortable feeling I have done my duty by them.'[4]

Despite noticeable developments in her Modernist techniques, as well as garnering international attention, Hodgkins, the dutiful daughter, felt pressured to return to her family. Her time in New Zealand, however, would not last for long. Eager to continue positioning her art within the international arena, in 1906, Hodgkins set sail again for Britain and Europe. During this second extended visit, Hodgkins set herself apart from the majority of her female peers by exhibiting alongside prominent avant-garde male artists, as well as starring in solo exhibitions. All the while, Hodgkins was resolute in searching for new possibilities to expand upon her earlier Impressionist experimentation. This is evident in her watercolour *At the Window* (Fig. 4), which presents a Modernist interest in the combination of a still life arranged before windows with a view onto the garden, while simultaneously employing an Impressionist interplay of light and shadows with rapid, broken brushstrokes. Hodgkins would continue to evolve the motif of *At the Window* into a more conceptualised method later in her oeuvre.

Upon Hodgkins' final but brief return to New Zealand in 1912, a local newspaper acknowledged the artist's international status, while also characterising its limitations: 'Miss Hodgkins has succeeded, has "arrived." A small success, yet a definite arrival.'[5] For Hodgkins, this proved to be more of a provocation than a solidification of her achievements. By now, she aligned her art with the European Modernists and considered her work to be more advanced than her fellow countrymen's: 'The French are so eager for new ideas; they give them such a welcome; and the progress must come with new ideas, mustn't it? We can't go on with modern minds painting like the old masters.'[6] Consequently, in 1913, Hodgkins left New Zealand for the last time. Only then would she be recognised for her contributions not just as a leading 'woman artist' but also as a distinguished Modernist in her own right, with a lasting legacy for the singularity of her aesthetic voice.

At the onset of the First World War, Hodgkins was forced to leave Paris, where she was the head of her own watercolour

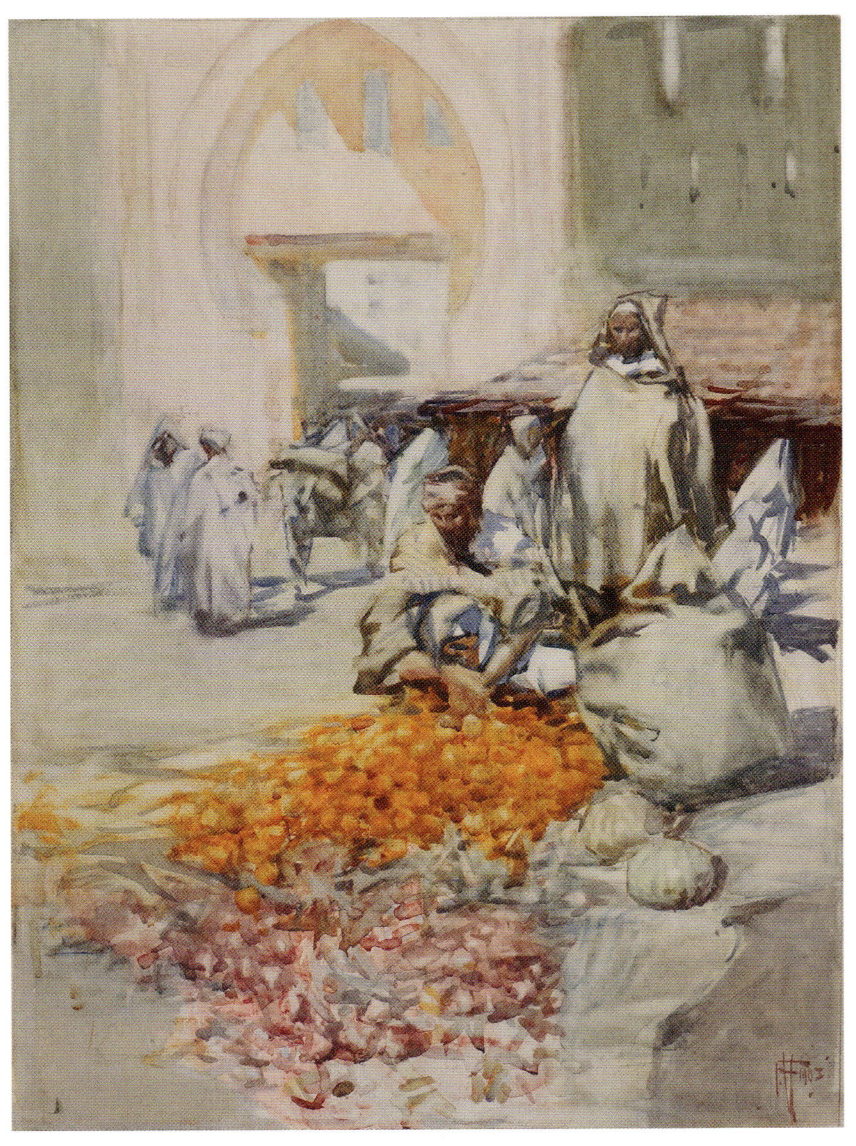

3. *The Orange Sellers, Tangier*, 1903, watercolour

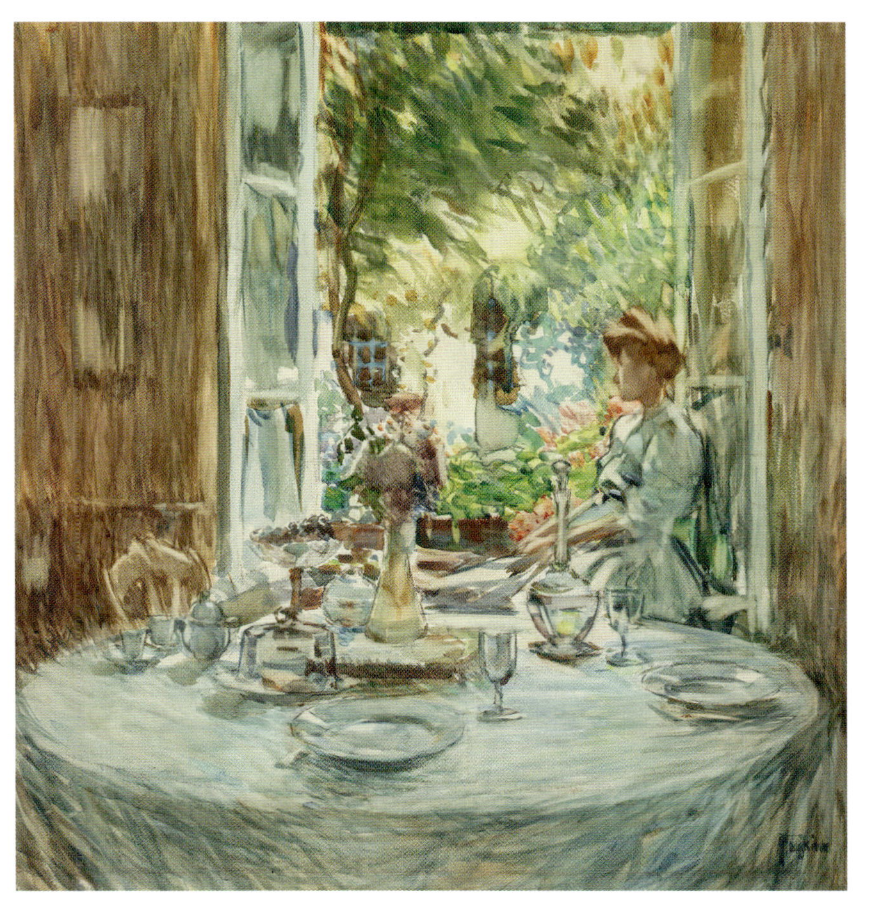

4. *At the Window, c.1912, watercolour*

school, a frequent exhibitor at galleries and enjoyed consistent involvement with exhibiting societies (for which she was
honoured with awards and flattering reviews in the press).[7]
During the war years, Hodgkins settled in St Ives, Cornwall,
after having previously painted in the British coastal art col-
onies of St Ives, Newlyn and Penzance at the turn of the
century. Feeling isolated from the vitality of her former life
amongst the Parisian avant-garde and her adoring students,
she wrote: 'I find I am too modern for people down here & I am
conscious of the cold eye of distrust & disapproval by the older
members of St Ives.'[8]

At this time, Hodgkins was restricted from natural, *en plein
air* painting, due to the wartime ban on coastal sketching.
Instead, her subjects consisted of studio-based portraiture.
The expressively dream-like portrait *Loveday and Ann: Two
Women with a Basket of Flowers* (Fig. 5) was exhibited at the
National Portrait Society in 1916. Unlike the other more traditional British society portraits in the exhibition, Hodgkins'
painting was different in both spirit and technique. Her delight
in the nineteenth-century Nabi artists such as Pierre Bonnard
and Édouard Vuillard is revealed through her depiction of two
sitters – the daughters of local fishermen; their unnatural
seafoam green-tinted skin blends into the decoratively patterned domestic environment. Interest in the decorative continued to be a major strain within twentieth-century British
Modernism, and Hodgkins' central placement of a basket of
bright flowers not only unites the stylised individuals but
also intensifies her use of an ornamental language. Although
the painting is in oil, Hodgkins treats the medium as if it
were her earlier watercolour method of ephemeral washes,
contributing to an instinctively free feeling of the overall composition. As Hodgkins rightly concluded, her modern portraits
were not yet understood by British critics of the time. One
detractor wrote: 'This is the exhibit of a pyrotechnic artist
in paint, it is not portraiture, or if it is, I never want to meet

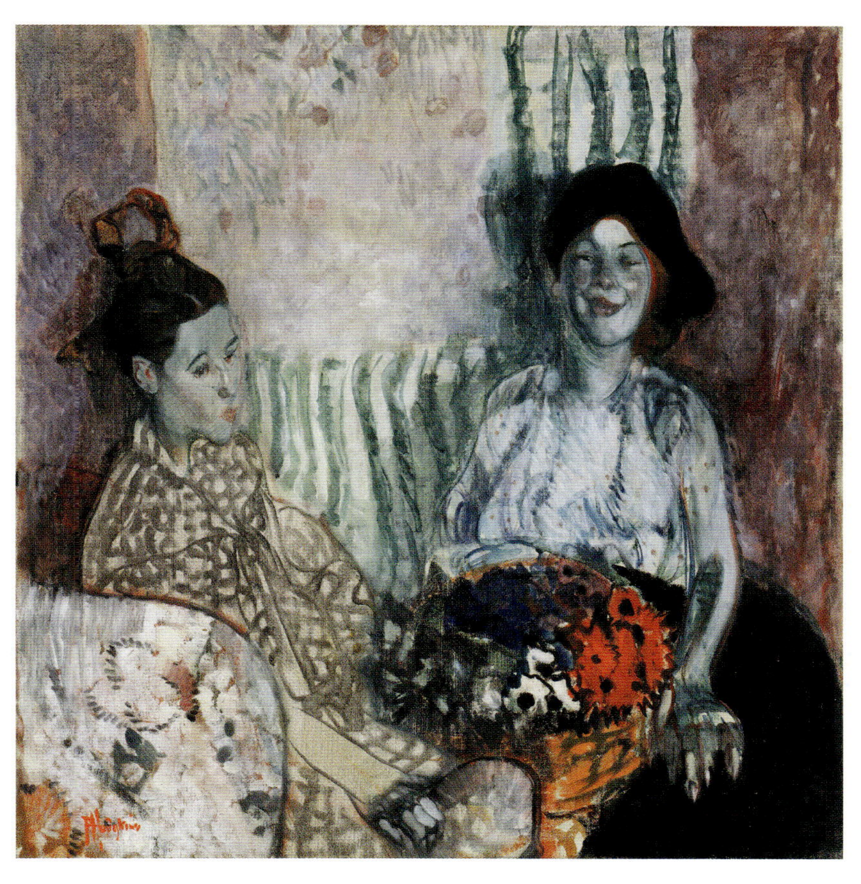

5. *Loveday and Ann: Two Women with a Basket of Flowers*, 1915, oil on canvas

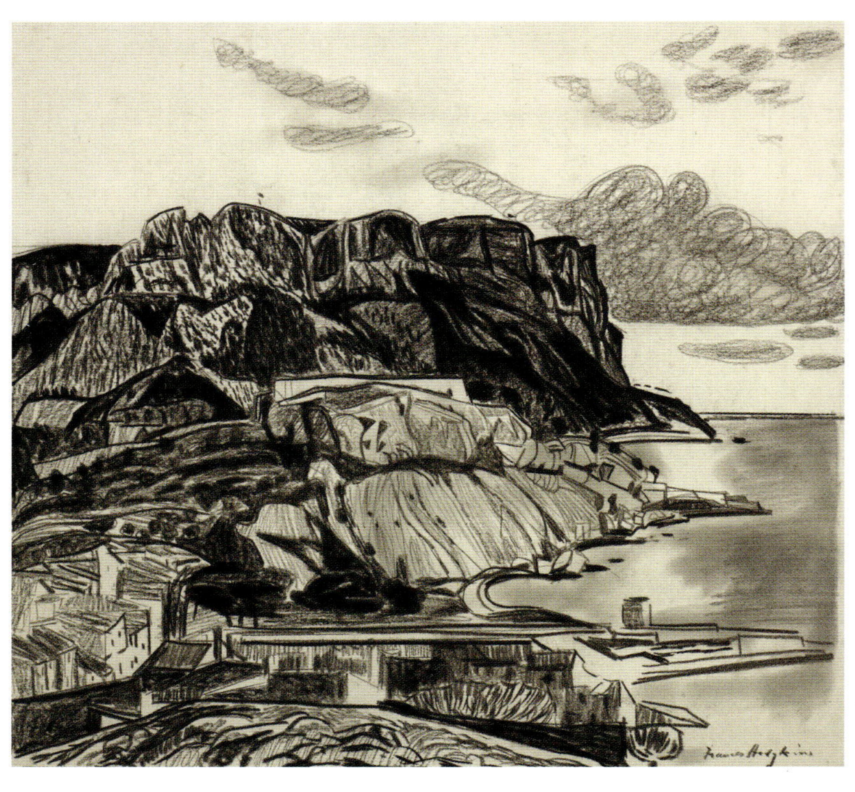

6. *Cassis*, c.1920–30, chalk

Loveday and Ann.'[9] It would not be until decades later, when Hodgkins' place in British Modernism was officially confirmed, that *Loveday and Ann* would be acquired by Britain's national collection of British art at the Tate in London. Delighted by the final acquisition of her work, Hodgkins wrote: 'It gives me intense pleasure to know that my picture is enshrined in glory at Millbank.'[10]

It was in her St Ives studio that Hodgkins developed her previous watercolour technique, moving from Impressionism (see Figs 2–4) to a definitive twentieth-century Modernist approach. She did so by experimenting with the principles of Post-Impressionism, as popularised by the English theorist, Clive Bell. In his book *Art* (1913), Bell urged artists to create from within themselves, so that their personal arrangements of volumes, lines, shapes and colours, may or may not reflect reality but would, nevertheless, encourage an emotional or even a spiritual response from the viewer.

By the end of the war, Hodgkins was no longer constrained to indoor work, and her peripatetic existence resumed in the 1920s, with sketching excursions to the provinces of France. Looking towards untamed nature for new ideas, Hodgkins' *Cassis* (Fig. 6) is one of many landscape chalk drawings she made during this period. Near to Marseilles, the fishing harbour with its imposing coastal cliffs inspired the artist to draw using a decisive black line, which was a response to the Post-Impressionist doctrines of Paul Cézanne. Hodgkins' tonal shading of the overlapping limestone precipices in a series of jagged planes contrasts with the subtly defined terraced meadows and a sun-bleached village in the lower-left foreground. The rhythmic modulations of form layered in *Cassis* suggest an immaterial almost mystical quality, which would define her later landscapes and serve as an influence over younger artists of the Neo-Romanticism movement.[11]

At this point in her career, Hodgkins not only demonstrated mastery in painting and drawing, but she also proved to be a

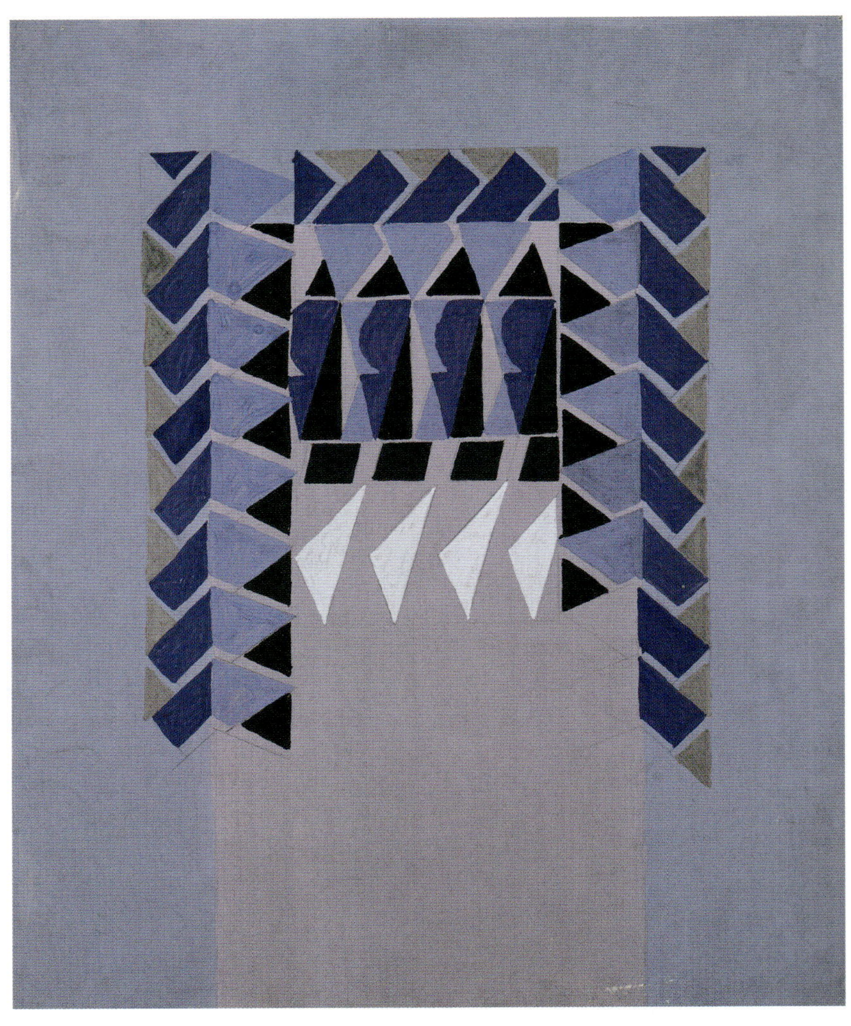

7. (above) *Untitled (Textile design, no. I)*, c.1925, gouache on paper
8. (opposite above) *Untitled (Textile design, no. IV)*, c.1925, gouache on paper
9. (opposite below) *Printed Textile (Block print on silk handkerchief)*,
c.1926, block print on silk

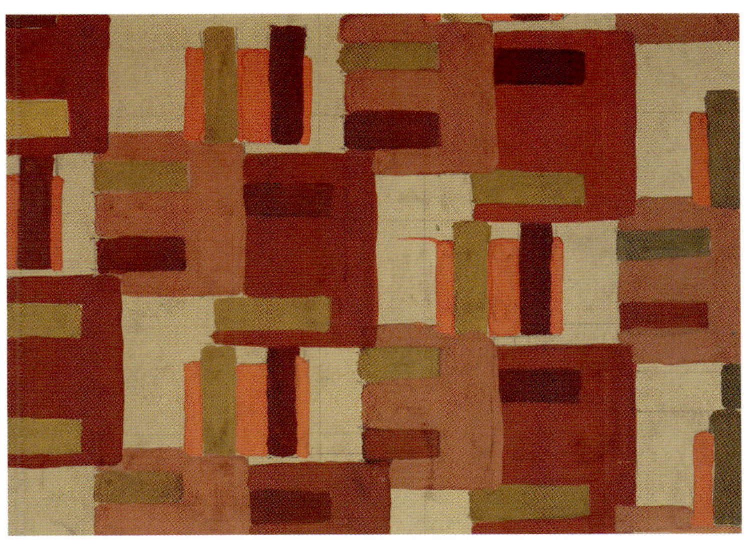

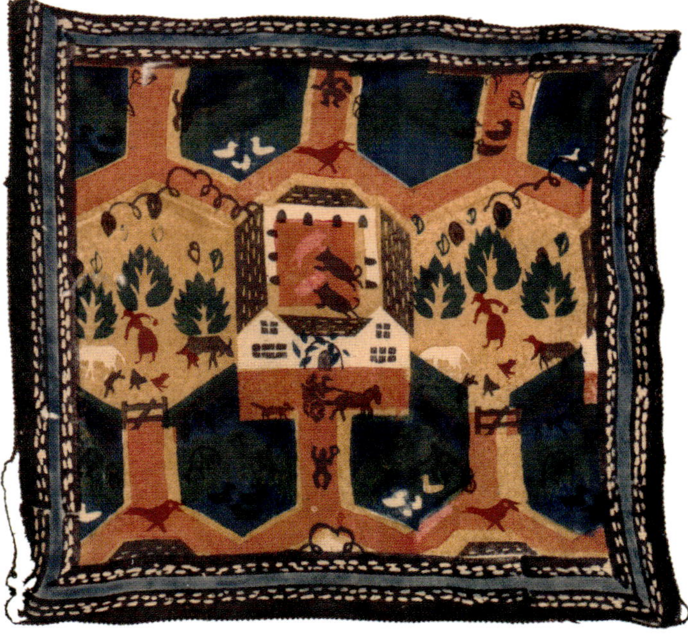

skilled textile designer. Despite modest working trips abroad, invariably staying in inexpensive lodgings, Hodgkins faced constant pecuniary troubles throughout the 1920s. Few of her works sold, as with other Modernists, during the bleak period of economic depression after the war. Close to abandoning her career in both Britain and Europe, Hodgkins booked a ticket back to Melbourne in 1925. At the last moment, she was offered employment as a fabric designer at the Calico Printers' Association (CPA) in Manchester. Few of Hodgkins' designs survive from this period, but those that do (Figs 7–8) feature Modernist concerns that she had previously experimented with in other media, such as expressive colour arrangements and deliberate abstraction.

Soon after she began her position, Hodgkins was sent to Paris to broaden her knowledge in design. It was there that she visited the *Exposition Internationale des Arts Décoratifs*, which she described as 'an ultra-modern Show ... all marvellously well done & displayed – that is all except the British Section, which quite failed to express itself in modern terms, & as a consequence looked old fashioned & dingy beside the faultless order & taste of France ...'[12] Returning to her work in Manchester, Hodgkins now drew from an array of new influences, including the formal elements found in the applied arts of Art Nouveau and Art Deco artists, as well as art connecting to her colonial roots. For instance, *Untitled (Textile design, no. I)* (Fig. 7), features Art Deco diamond patterning and resembles the rectangular units of warm tones seen in *Untitled (Textile design, no. IV)* (Fig. 8). Both are reminiscent of the geometric designs and earthy colours of the *tapa*, or bark, cloth found in the rich history of Antipodean and Polynesian art.[13]

During the twentieth century, British Modernists believed that modern art ought to have an all-over decorative effect – that is, flat fields of patterns rather than illusionistic representations, as prompted by artist, critic and theorist Roger Fry in his book *Vision and Design* (1920). Hodgkins' emphasis on a strikingly decorative composition led to the design of a silk handkerchief – *Printed Textile* (Fig. 9). Even though the motif is representational, the subject maintains a graphic quality, with its symmetrical setting filled with silhouettes of stylised animals and figures in a farm. Having earned enough of an income to continue painting in Britain, Hodgkins left the CPA after six months, since she was eager to 'escape the tedium of textiles . . .' and the 'monotonous life of a designer'.[14]

Hodgkins' art gained substantial recognition within the British Modernist movement during the late 1920s and into the 1930s. In 1927 she exhibited in the London Group and the New English Art Club – two societies offering exhibiting opportunities besides the RA – and in 1929 she was elected to join the avant-garde Seven and Five Society, which originally started as a group of seven painters and five sculptors. Beyond group exhibitions, Hodgkins held one-woman shows, one of which took place at the St George's Gallery, London, and served as the true catalyst for her artistic career, thereafter. The owner of the Gallery, Arthur R. Howell, was interested in young, emerging contemporary artists, but at the advanced age of 61, Hodgkins finally received her first contract to be represented by Howell from 1928 to 1931. The dealer's agreement would guarantee Hodgkins a small but consistent form of income for the first time in her professional life. This granted her with a sense of security and freedom to continue developing her landscapes and still life paintings on excursions abroad.

Hodgkins' preferred subjects during this period were still life studies of form, influenced by Cubists such as Pablo Picasso. However, she reinvented this centuries-old genre by uniting still life and landscape, which Hodgkins characterised as 'open-air still life'.[15] Diverging from the predominantly interior settings of earlier examples in the art historical canon, Hodgkins assumed a distinct approach by transforming her still lifes into variant landscapes. An example of this repositioning can

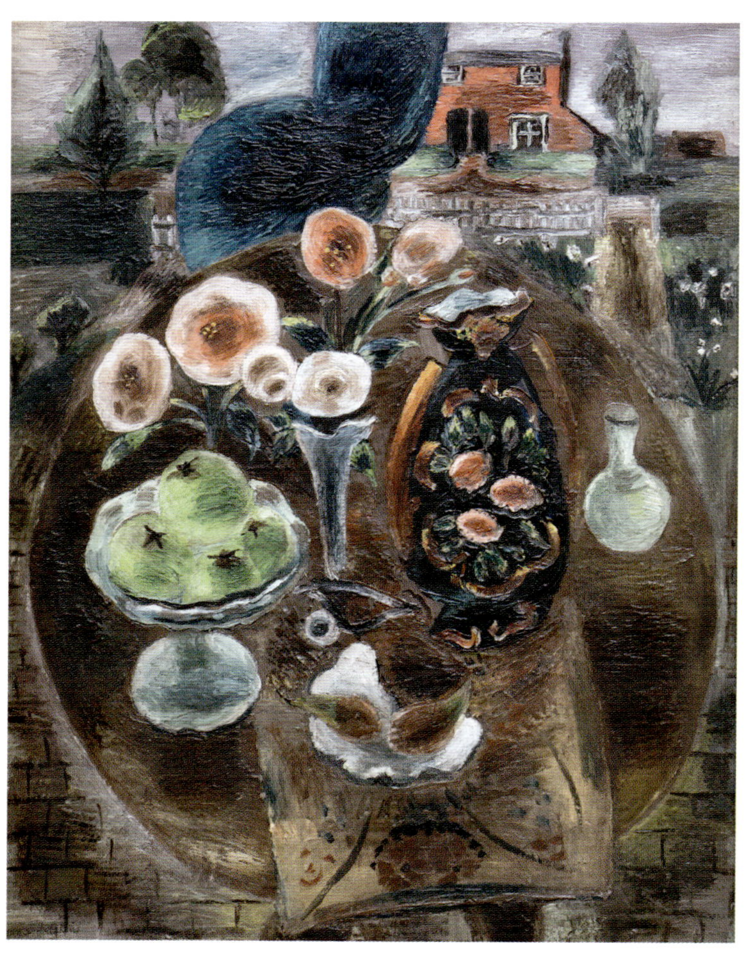

10. *Still Life*, 1929, oil on canvas

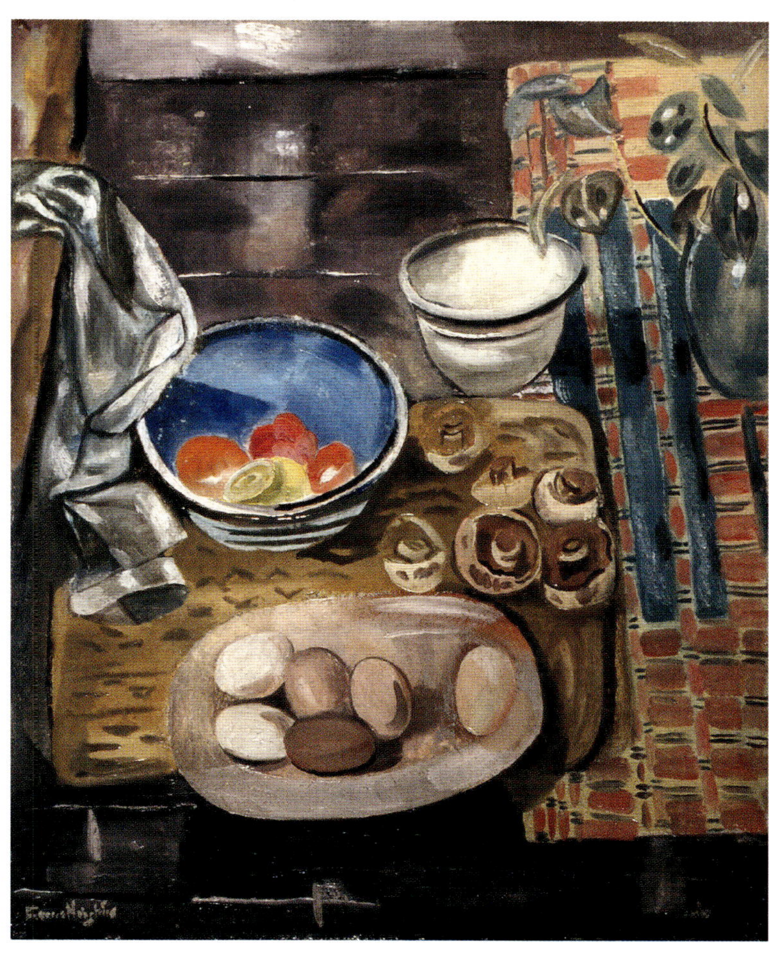

11. *Still Life: Eggs, Tomatoes and Mushrooms*, c.1929, oil on canvas

be seen with the table in *Still Life* (Fig. 10), which has been moved outside into an English pastoral scene, with a redbrick country house in the background. In *Still Life*, Hodgkins reconciles unusual spatial concepts by tilting and foreshortening the perspective of the still life, filling the majority of the composition to the point of almost being parallel to the picture surface. This Modernist method of framing is also evident in *Still Life: Eggs, Tomatoes and Mushrooms* (Fig. 11), which again is presented from the artist's idiosyncratic use of an aerial viewpoint. In this oil painting, a narrative unfolds as interactions between the tightly organised ingredients of a vegetarian English breakfast are analysed. A white Cézannesque cloth directs attention to the leading characters centred in the foreground: a bowl of sliced tomatoes, strewn mushrooms and a platter of eggs. Hodgkins reinterpreted still lifes by assimilating Cubist doctrines into her own work.

Building upon her earlier employment as a textile designer, the incorporation of rippling fabrics became an important element in Hodgkins' still life motif throughout the 1930s. *Red Jug* (Fig. 12) continues the theme of her *plein air* still lifes, but now the fabric becomes an essential element of the arrangement alongside the urn and vase of arum lilies, as the cloth extends across the entire composition. The function of fabric heightens the subject's sense of depth, as one draped end close to the picture plane flutters beyond the table of objects, leading to the surrounding landscape and striated sky. In *Still Life with Fruit Dishes* (Fig. 13), the tablecloth rises vertically and surrealistically supports an otherwise heavy burden of fruits, flowers, vases and jugs, as the mass of objects hovers in space. *Still Life with Red Jar* (Fig. 14) can be interpreted as the culmination of Hodgkins' fusion of still life with fabric. In this work, a semi-transparent undulating sheet, with touches of mauve and violet, partially obscures an assortment of articles, while simultaneously unifying the composition into one complete expression of the inner spirit of the still life.

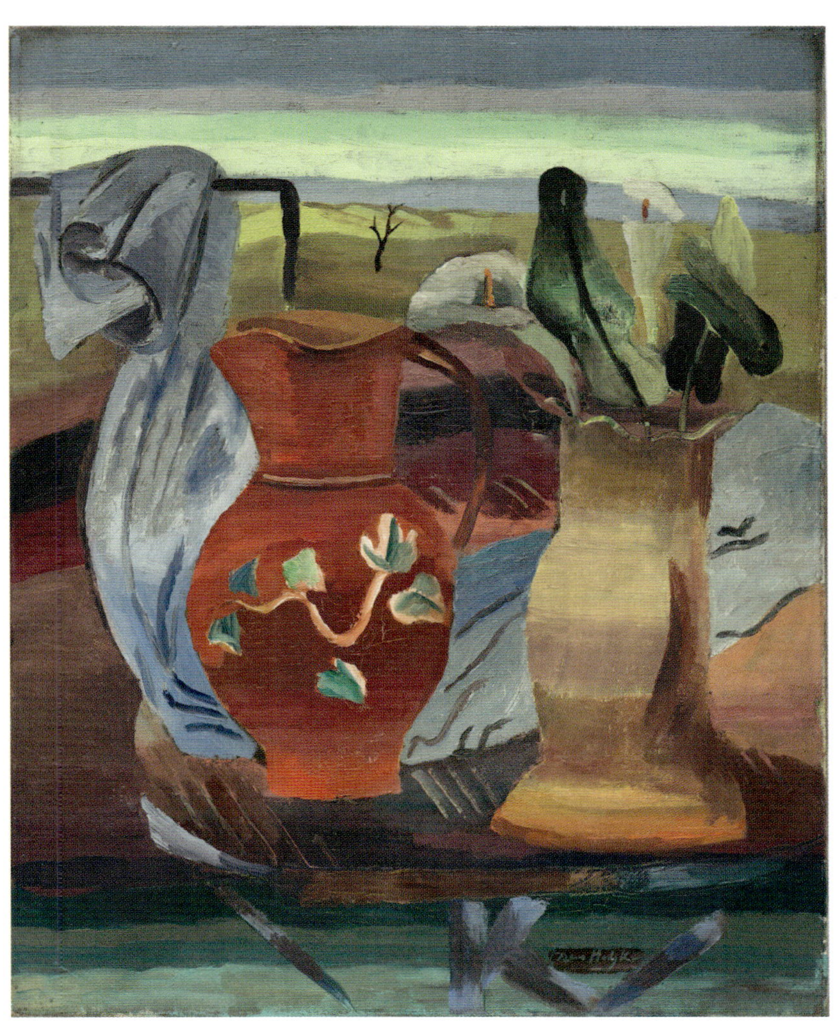

12. *Red Jug*, 1931, oil on canvas

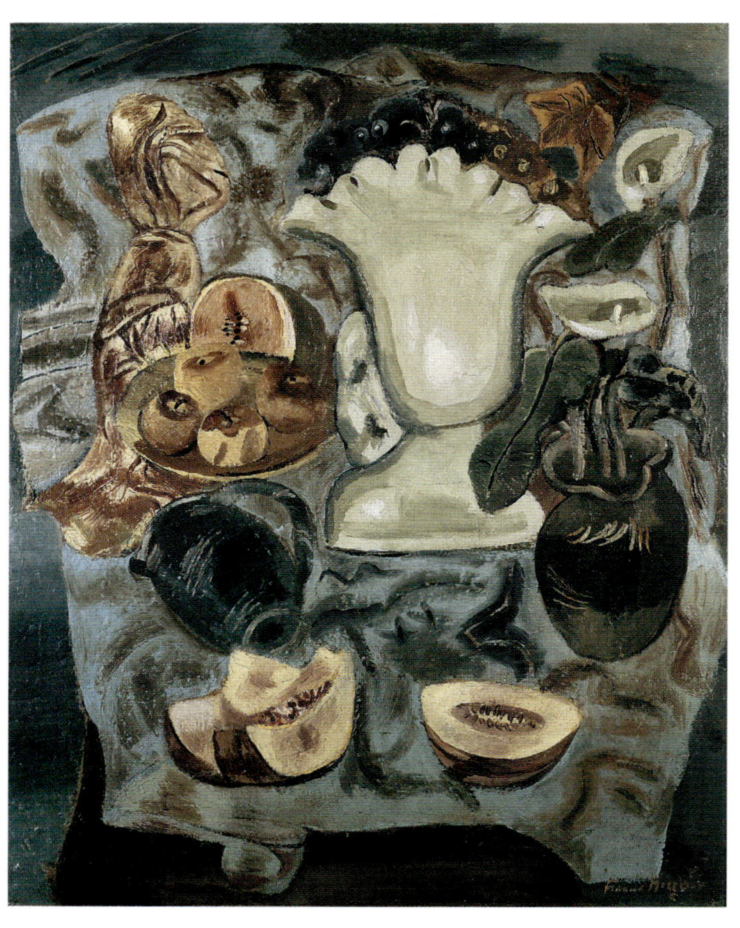

13. *Still Life with Fruit Dishes*, c.1931–7, oil on canvas laid on hardboard

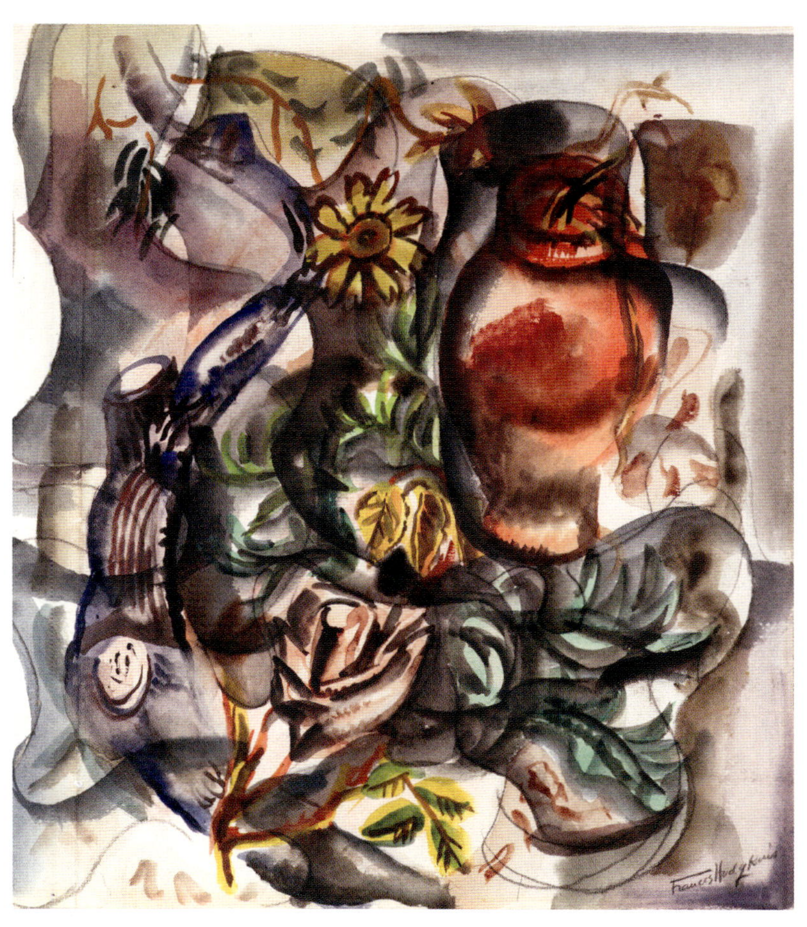

14. *Still Life with Red Jar*, c.1933, watercolour

Hodgkins' Femininity

As her career in Britain developed, Hodgkins became increasingly involved in an interconnected web of young male British artists, and her friendships were strengthened with men such as Cedric Morris, Paul Nash, Graham Sutherland and John Piper. For instance, after their initial meeting in 1917 at Newlyn in Cornwall, Hodgkins' and Morris' lives were constantly intertwined. At the time that Hodgkins painted *Still Life: Eggs, Tomatoes and Mushrooms* (see Fig. 11), she was Morris' houseguest; while Morris frequently sub-let Hodgkins' studio in London. Both exhibited together in the Seven and Five Society, and their work was often selected for the same shows. On multiple occasions, they travelled together on painting excursions, attended each other's exhibitions, socialised in the same bohemian circles and also shared patrons. While Morris admired Hodgkins as 'a completely original' painter, Hodgkins received financial assistance from Morris.[16] Hodgkins confirmed her gratitude when she wrote: '. . . the fact that I am working here today – in a state of comparative liberty & independence I very largely owe to the friendship of . . . Cedric.'[17]

To commemorate their friendship, both artists painted portraits of one another. Morris, who was 20 years her junior, painted Hodgkins aged 59 in *Portrait of Frances Hodgkins* (Fig. 15). This intimate, but not particularly flattering, portrait portrays Hodgkins in a realistic manner, marked by the inevitable signs of aging: swollen eyes, sagging jowls and her 'Titian'-coloured dark red wig, which she wore to appear younger.[18] In return, Hodgkins painted Morris and his macaw, Rubio, in *Cedric Morris (Man with Macaw)* (Fig. 16) with a Modernist methodology, revealing her perception of the sitter's inner essence rather than a detailed likeness.

Hodgkins painted this portrait during one of her visits to Pound Farm, the estate of Morris and his partner, Arthur Lett-Haines, near Higham, Suffolk. In this work, she linked

Morris' identity to his Arcadian existence, removed from the fast-paced London art world. To Morris and to other artists across the whole country, working both in the countryside and in London's urban sprawl, Hodgkins became an influential leader for the revelatory nature of her uniquely individual style. Hodgkins' countless achievements and powerful influence were ultimately rooted in her unconventional life journey from a Victorian colonial Impressionist past to her fearless travelling around the world as an avant-garde Modernist. Myfanwy Evans wrote about this transition, in which Hodgkins freed herself from the past: 'The present affected her transitorially – she shook the cocoon threads of influence off steadily, year by year, until, at about sixty, she emerged as a butterfly, unlike any known species of butterfly save in her brilliance and her delicacy.' Evans continued:

> But England was beginning, in spite of herself, to grow upon her and when the second world war forced her once more to remain here, she was able to bring all the intensity of France and Spain, all the brilliance of that New Zealand light and all the boldness of her Parisian-learnt colour to glow within the subtleties of an English mist. She had only to paint the broken implements in a deserted farm-yard or the moss-grown curve of a mill-wheel, to say all that she needed to say about herself and England.[19]

Hodgkins continued to expand her Modernist expressions in paintings such as *Wings over Water* (Fig. 17) by reintroducing the framing method of positioning a still life against a window (as in her earlier more Impressionist-inspired work, *At the Window*; see Fig. 4). Unlike Hodgkins' previous watercolour, however, *Wings over Water* reveals fluidity between the interior and the external view of Bodinnick, Cornwall. The artist blended the fore, middle and background by transposing natural life into the human sphere – seashells, potted plants and a flower-filled vase – and incorporated Modernist perspectival techniques. The middle-ground transitions to a parrot perched on a picket

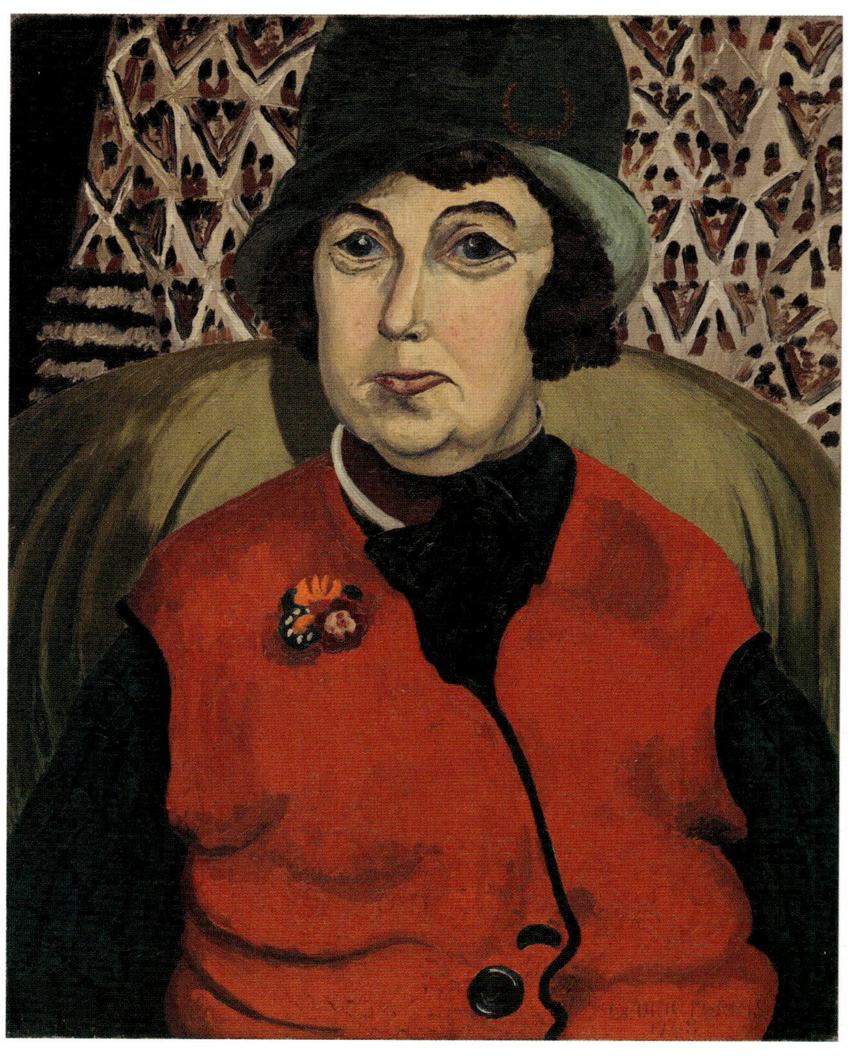

15. Cedric Morris, *Portrait of Frances Hodgkins*, 1928, oil on canvas

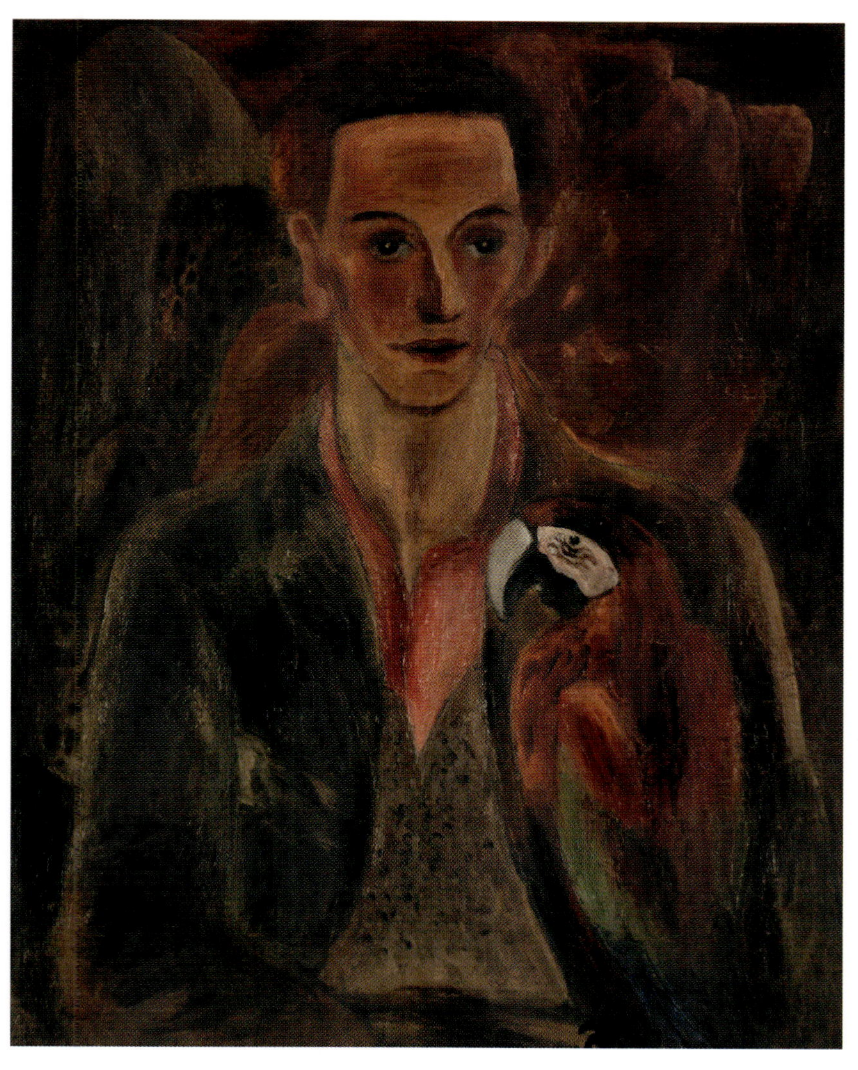

16. *Portrait of Cedric Morris (Man with Macaw)*, 1930, oil on canvas

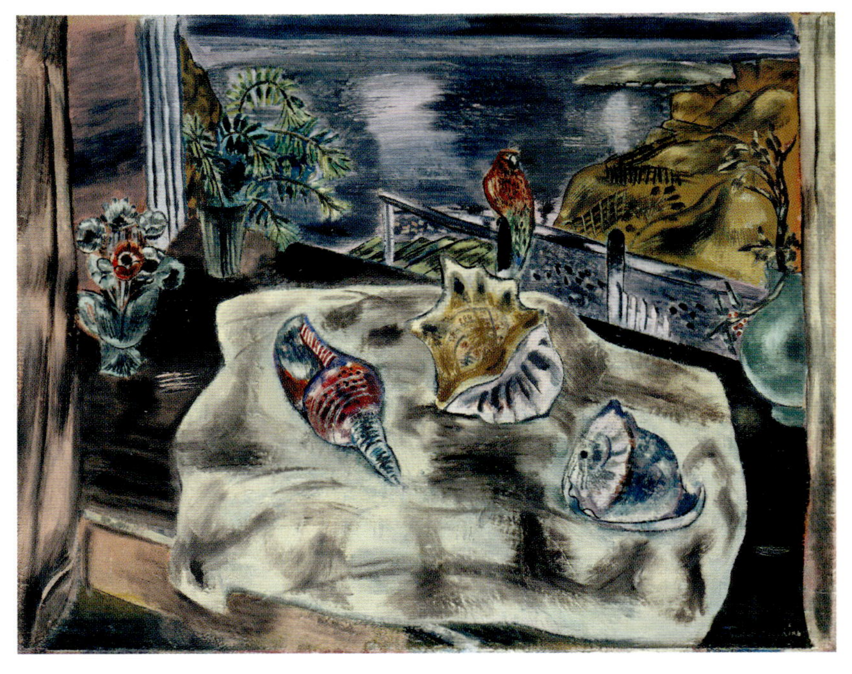

17. *Wings over Water*, 1930, oil on canvas

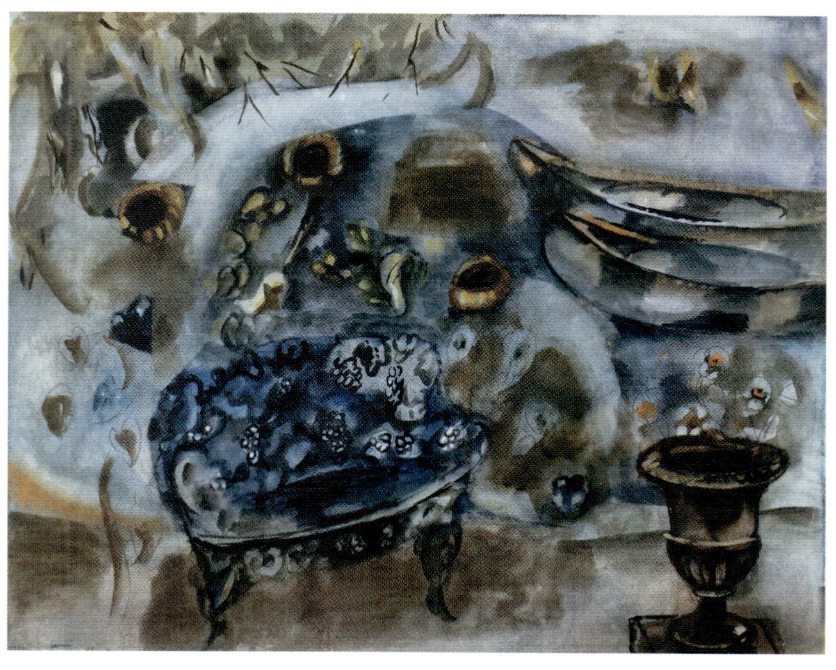

18. *The Lake (or River Garden Bridgnorth)*, c.1930–5, gouache on paper

fence, while the sea extends beyond. Similar to her technique in the portrait *Loveday and Ann* (see Fig. 5), Hodgkins' loose brushwork of thin, shimmering layers of paint, as if the medium were watercolour, combines separate components into one continuous whole. Finally, the interior is brightly lit with an artificial source of lighting, which spills into the darkened seascape. A glowing luminosity is also present in *The Lake (or River Garden Bridgnorth)* (Fig. 18) and in *Pleasure Garden* (Fig. 19). In these works, Hodgkins fuses separate components – such as the blue bench, sunflowers and urn in *The Lake*, or the still life in the veranda of *Pleasure Garden* – into harmoniously unified compositions with her delicate yet unorthodox merging of subtle colour modulations.

Although Hodgkins had established her base in England since 1913, she continued to travel throughout the 1930s. One destination, which enhanced her landscape practice, was Ibiza, with its Balearic cliffs, wild beaches and dense forests. Hodgkins' *Spring in the Ravine* (Fig. 20), painted during sunset's transformative light, demonstrates her mastery as an effective colourist. In this painting, her employment of iridescent pinks and blues transforms a conventional landscape into an experimental one. Hodgkins' use of Neo-Primitivism to flatten forms and compress the pictorial space is similar to the works of Cornish folk painter, Alfred Wallis. Her surreal colour arrangements, emphasis on design and free treatment of an anthropomorphically shaped landscape prefigure Neo-Romanticism. *Road to the hills, Ibiza* (Fig. 21) presents a more recognisable Mediterranean landscape, with tree-clad sandy hills. In this watercolour, Hodgkins painted using dynamic calligraphic strokes to delineate different features of the land in black, while creating a contrast with the empty white of the paper. Hodgkins' sophisticated use of abstraction in these Ibizan landscapes was later translated into her paintings of post-war ruins found in the English countryside.

Throughout these years, her work gained steady recognition. Although Hodgkins was conscious of her status as a 'woman artist', she refused to disguise her female self like several of her British contemporaries, such as the Constructivist Marlow Moss (for more information about Marlow Moss, see the third book in this Modern Women Artists series) or the abstract sculptor Barbara Hepworth. Hodgkins also struggled with the fact that she was older than the majority of those she exhibited with, for instance, all of the members of the Seven and Five Society, including: Ivon Hitchens and Winifred Nicholson, whose still life work also explored the relationship between inner and outer spaces.[20]

In order to reconcile her identity as an older 'woman artist', Hodgkins produced poignant self-portraits: *Still Life: Self-Portrait* (Fig. 22) and *Self Portrait: Still Life* (Fig. 23). The absence of Hodgkins' physicality attests to her inextricable link to these paintings through metaphorical rather than literal associations. Hodgkins' intention with these unconventional portraits was to direct the viewer's attention away from the self-conscious artist and instead to her art.

Contrary to the doctrines of Modernism, Hodgkins embedded feminine tropes into these works such as her choice of colours – rose, blush and magenta – and her selection of possessions: a red beret, a handbag, scarves, shoes, belts, brightly patterned textiles, flowers, vases and a reflection-less mirror. In these self-portraits, Hodgkins reconstructed her experience of womanhood by cultivating a uniquely feminine modern style that was far different from what has been deemed as more masculine forms of geometric abstraction, as found in the non-objective art of Ben Nicholson, for instance. However, several art critics, who asserted a discourse of Modernism as masculine, dismissed Hodgkins' radical self-portraits as too 'feminine in character'.[21] Hodgkins' self-portraits were resistant to historical categorisation, fitting neither the genre of portraiture nor that of the still life. Other critics, such as Eric Hall McCormick, were intrigued, noting: 'The so-called self-portrait – a still life of her personal belongings – is a sly evasion, a sophisticated, elegant joke.'[22]

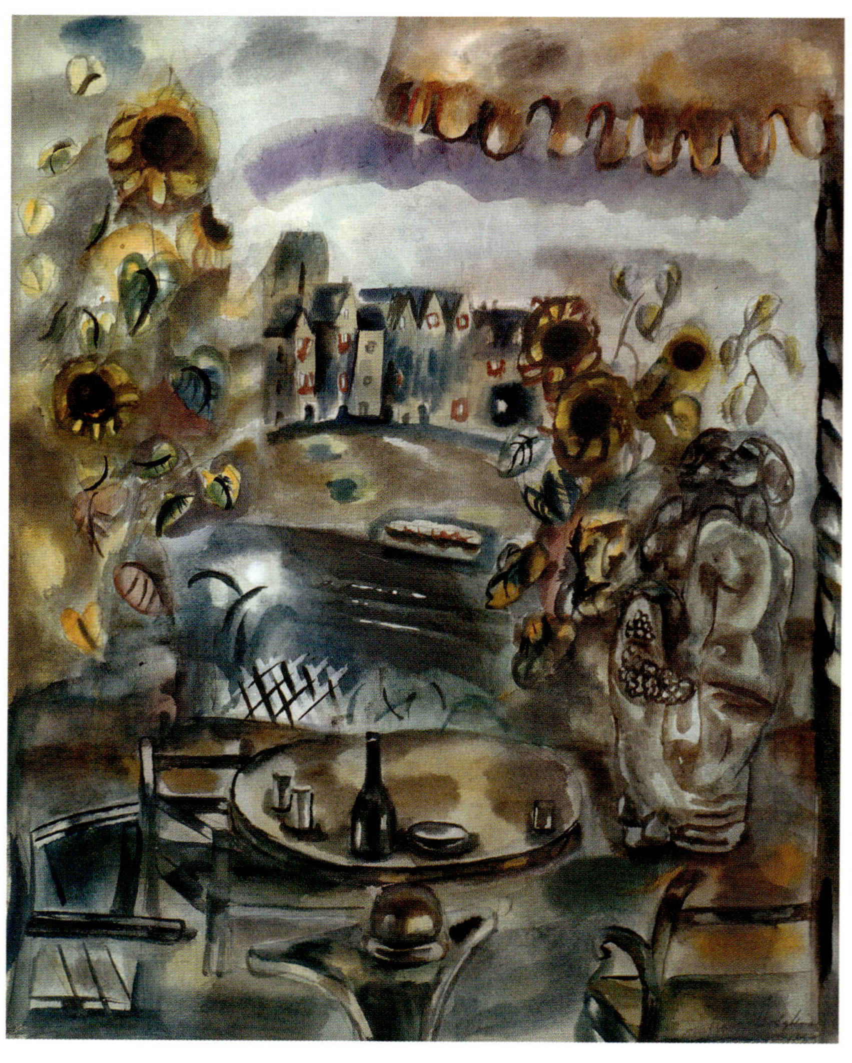

19. (above) *Pleasure Garden*, 1932, watercolour
20. (opposite above) *Spring in the Ravine*, c.1933, oil on canvas
21. (opposite below) *Road to the hills, Ibiza*, 1933, watercolour

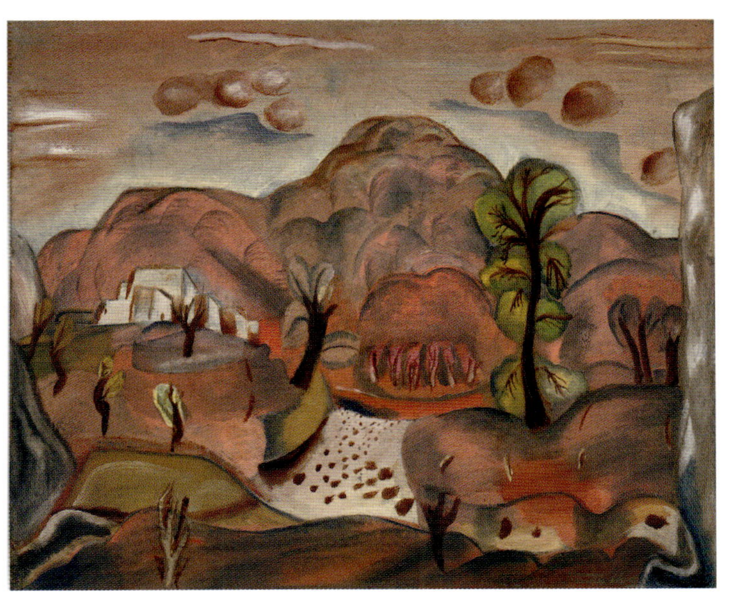

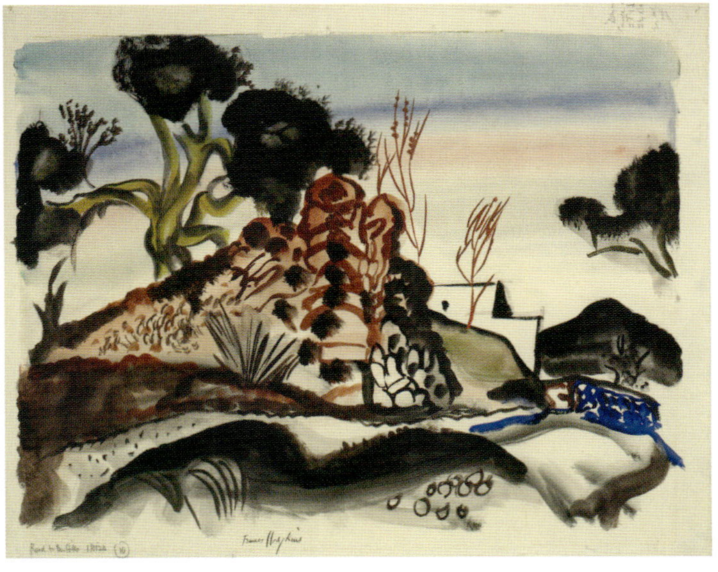
Frances Hodgkins

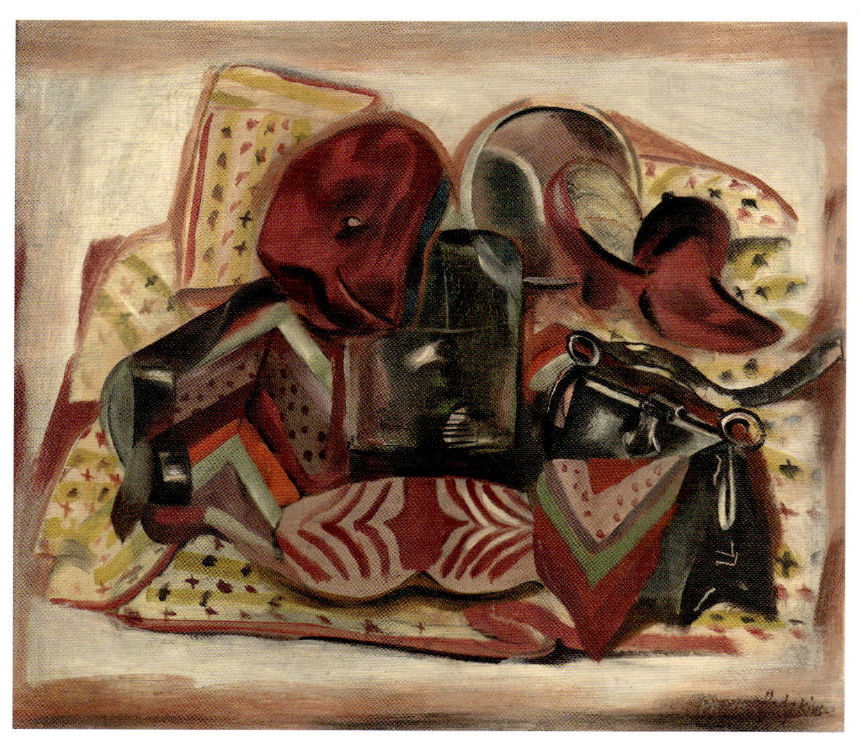

22. *Still Life: Self-Portrait*, c.1935, oil on panel

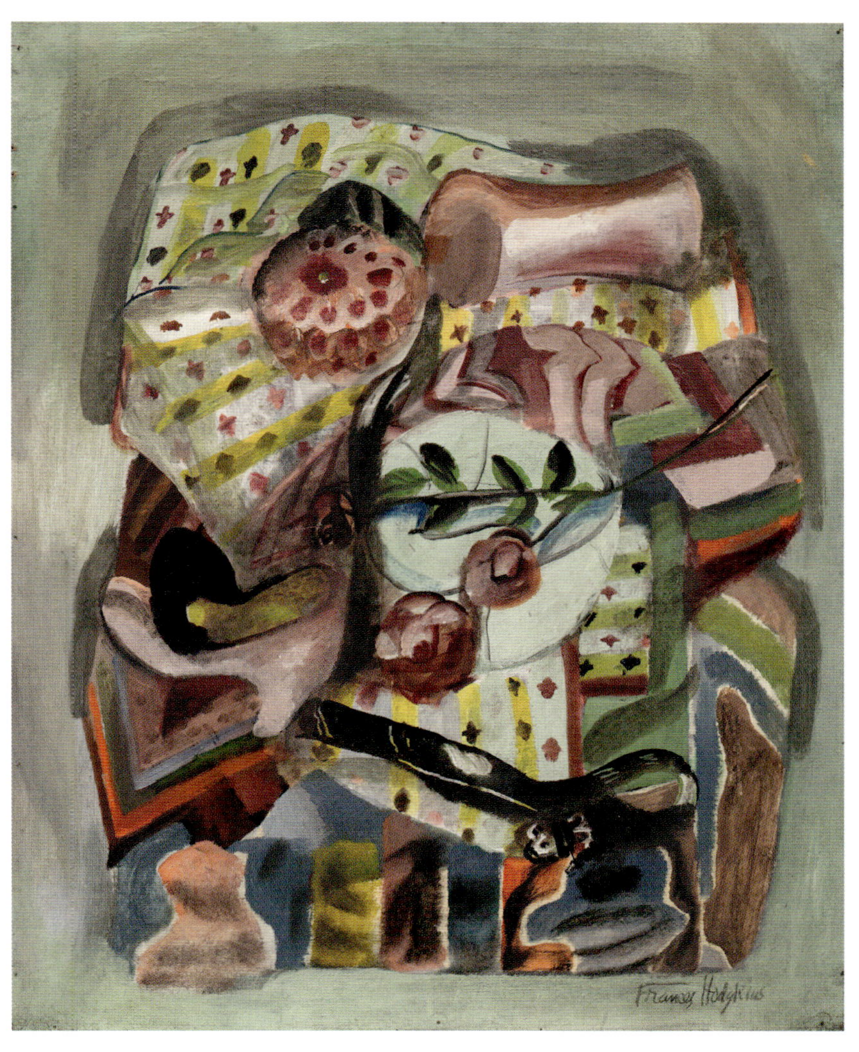

23. *Self Portrait: Still Life*, c.1935, oil on cardboard

Hodgkins as a Neo-Romantic Modernist

Hodgkins continued her still life works surrounded by landscapes but with a heightened sense of the uncanny, as prominently found in the early twentieth-century movement known as Surrealism. Hodgkins painted *Pumpkins and Pimenti* (Fig. 24) at a time when Surrealism was becoming increasingly present. In 1936, British works were displayed alongside the main European founders of the movement in the *International Surrealist Exhibition* in London. Having already explored the subject of fruits and vegetables in *The Orange Sellers, Tangier*, Hodgkins transformed her Impressionist style into a paradigm of the modern still life with *Pumpkins and Pimenti*. In this unearthly, ethereal arrangement of grey, white and blue, any sense of realistic recession into depth is replaced by a rhythmic pattern that conveys a lively energy.

Hodgkins' late work, from the last decade of her life, has been identified as her most inventive and prefigured what came to be recognised as her Neo-Romantic tendency of the 1940s. Neo-Romanticism, a British modern movement, looked back to aspects of eighteenth- and nineteenth-century Romanticism in its reinterpretation of what has been regarded as 'visionary' landscapes by artists such as William Blake and Samuel Palmer. No longer looking for foreign muses, Hodgkins found inspiration in the British countryside. While staying with her friend and fellow artist John Piper, Hodgkins developed a motif of landscapes composed of colourful orchestrations of warped mechanical debris. Rather than still lifes featuring flowers, fruits and fabrics, Hodgkins now discovered beauty in powerful groupings of twentieth-century relics, creating a truly singular approach to modern still life–landscape painting. Hodgkins highlighted the 'spirit of the place' of *Quarry Farm, Wiltshire* (Fig. 25) by focusing less on the exact physicality of the landscape and more on the disused objects which define it (wheelbarrows, carts and a water tank) – all seen from

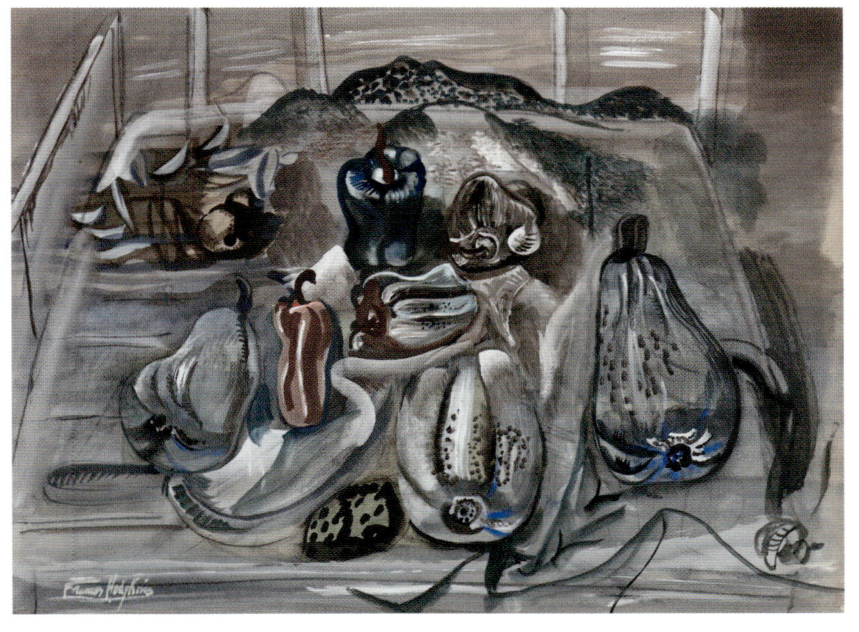

24. *Pumpkins and Pimenti*, c.1935–6, gouache, pencil and chalk

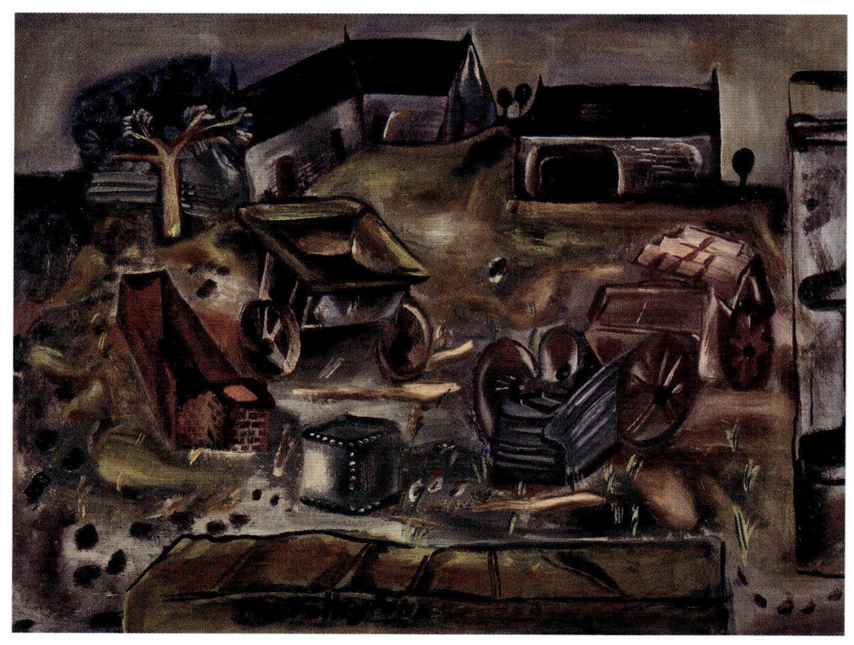

25. *Quarry Farm, Wiltshire, c.1937*, oil on canvas

an aerial perspective. Piper admired Hodgkins' subjects of
'. . . farm implements in disuse or dereliction . . .', later writing
that these paintings were '. . . of the times and timeless . . .'
in that 'they . . . are about humanity and its fate.'[23]

Hodgkins also enjoyed Welsh landscapes made up 'of steep
valleys speedy rivers & castles looking like their own mountains',[24] as can be seen in *Study for Pembrokeshire Landscape*
(Fig. 26). In this gouache, the blue-tinged mountains, naïvely
painted houses, an inflatable-like bridge, a rushing river and
cows delineated with just a few brushstrokes are all portrayed
in a deceptively simple, flattened way, evoking the faux-naïf
techniques Hodgkins had encountered when exhibiting with
the Seven and Five Society.

Well into the Second World War, Hodgkins retreated from
her painting excursions around Britain and rented a repur-
posed chapel as a studio in Corfe Castle, a village in Dorset.
During this time, Hodgkins developed a consciously romantic
sensibility, including elements from Neo-Romanticism and dis-
tortions of faux-naïveté. *Courtyard, Corfe Castle* (Fig. 27)
serves as a synthesis of these styles. The village, ranging from
barn structures to a fortified castle, possesses a barely recognisable quality verging on the eerie, due to wartime's harrow-
ing influence, as well as Hodgkins' captivation with ruins. Her
use of chalky white, and her deliberate choice of gouache,
highlights the spontaneous graphic effects Hodgkins previously
experimented with in *Pumpkins and Pimenti*. In the immediate
foreground, the presence of two tall plants, almost the same
scale of the structures, mark the mood as primal, or even
otherworldly. The disquiet of wartime can also be sensed in
the ambiguously anthropomorphic appearance of twentieth-
century debris found in *Broken Tractor* (Fig. 28). The discarded
tractor is reminiscent of the surrealistic objects in *Quarry Farm,
Wiltshire*, but this time the setting is wholly Neo-Romantic, as

26. (overleaf) *Study for Pembrokeshire Landscape*, 1938, gouache

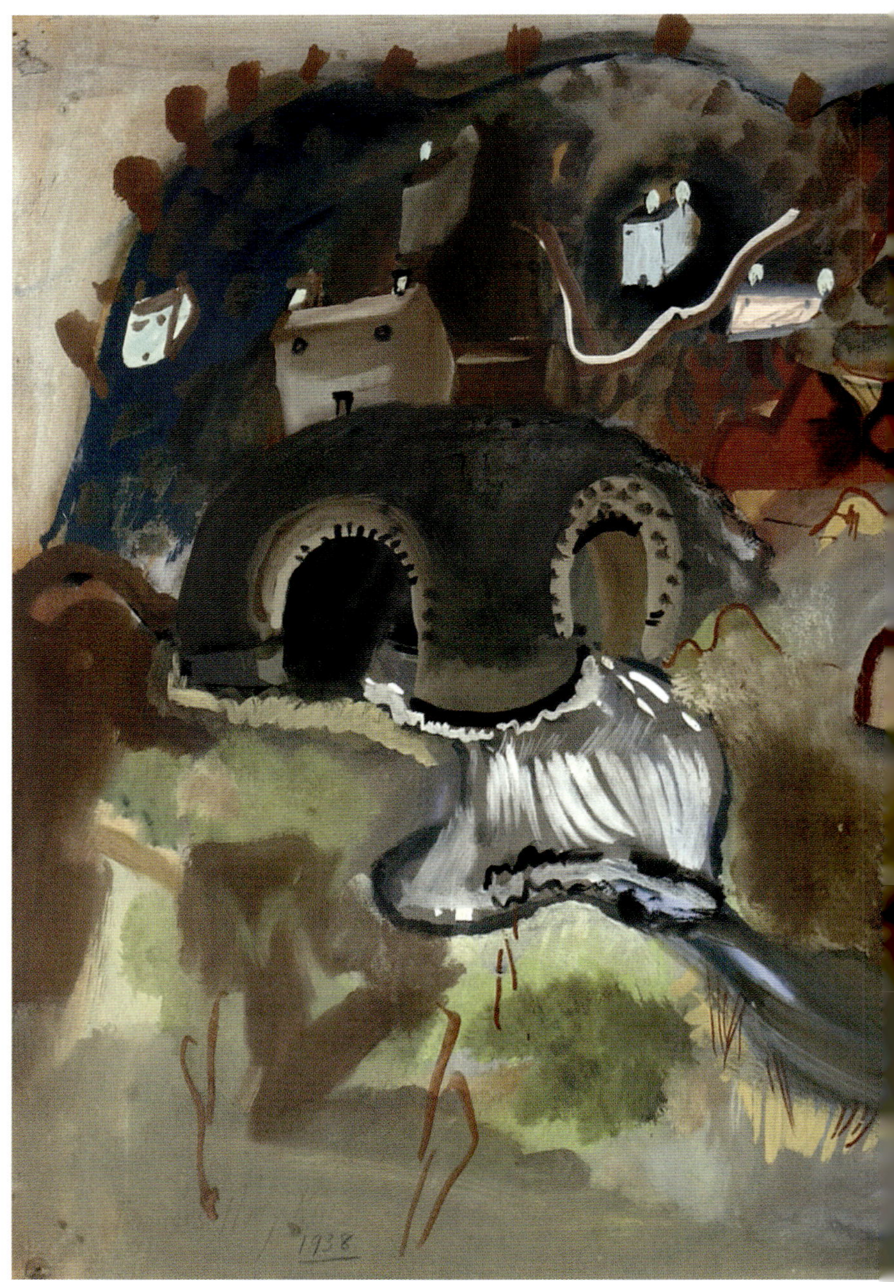

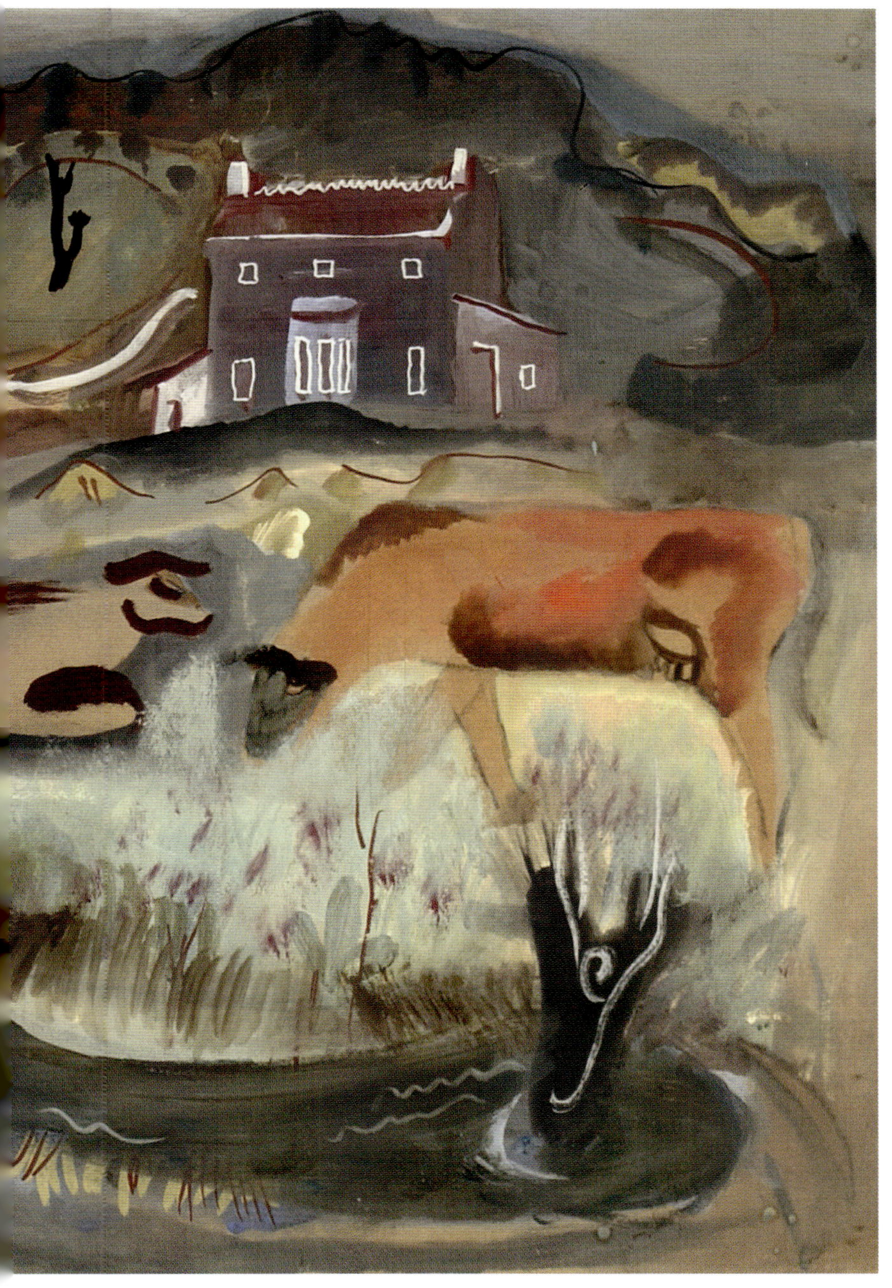

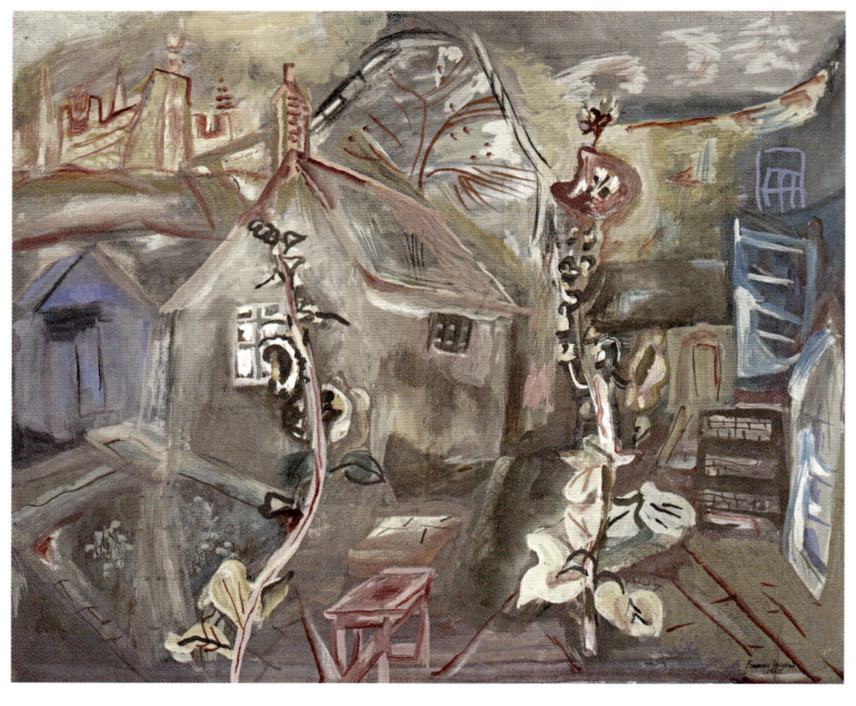

27. *Courtyard, Corfe Castle*, 1942, gouache, ink and charcoal

an edifice with a darkened cross looms in the distance along-side the ruins of perhaps an abbey or graveyard.

In the same year as *Courtyard, Corfe Castle* and *Broken Tractor* were painted, Piper published *British Romantic Artists*, in which he outlined eighteenth- and nineteenth-century British Romantic painting up until the work of Frances Hodgkins. In Piper's book, Hodgkins was described as a 'subjective paint-er whose harmonies of colour have their origins in Wiltshire farmyards, Welsh hills and Dorset coves.'[25] At the same time, eminent art historian, Sir Kenneth Clark advocated for the inclusion of Hodgkins in *The Penguin Modern Painters* series, which aimed to showcase painters to a wider public from 1944 to 1959. Evans, the only female author of the series, was to write the book, and Hodgkins was pleased: 'As far as pictures can be described no one could do it better ... Between us, your words & my painting go well together.'[26] However, due to war-time's unfavourable circumstances, publication was delayed, and Hodgkins grew apprehensive. She wrote, 'I should like to know if my Book is included in the main group Sutherland – Piper – or something slightly different *with other women* ...'[27]

After receiving recognition in the male-dominated art world, Hodgkins did not want to be marginalised as a 'woman artist', since at this time women's art was often considered as deriva-tive, following in the footsteps of their 'male superiors'. Never-theless, Hodgkins contributed to a new meaning of the 'modern woman artist'. Not only did she challenge manifestations of Modernist masculinity with her abstractions of decorative ornamentation, but she also wrestled with obstacles involving her life experiences as a woman. She replaced traditional nine-teenth- and twentieth-century values of women in society as maternal, domestic figures with the identity of a free-spirited, avant-garde artist. Having exhibited extensively in Britain and abroad, with an invitation to represent British art in the *Bien-nale di Venezia* in 1940, Hodgkins, now in her seventies, finally achieved a confirmed place in British Modernism. Her elevated

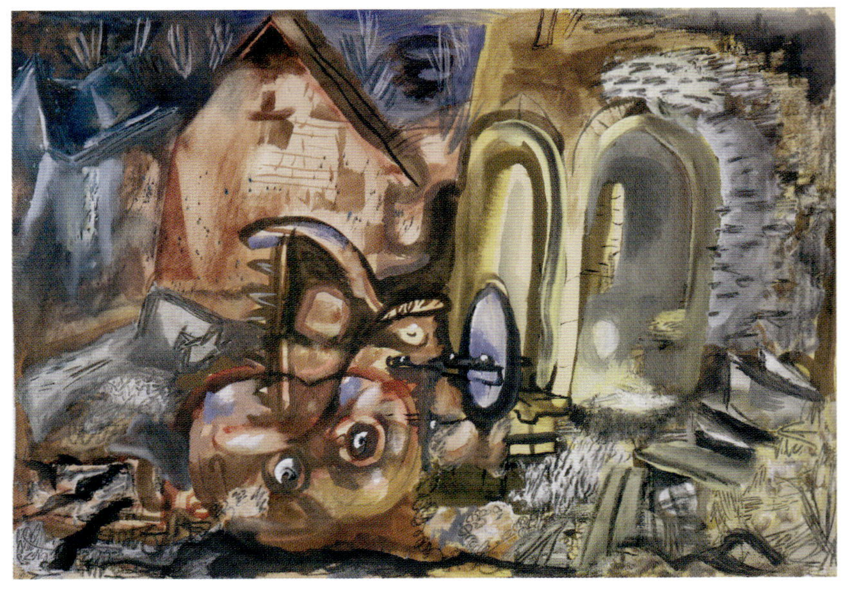

28. *Broken Tractor*, 1942, gouache on paper

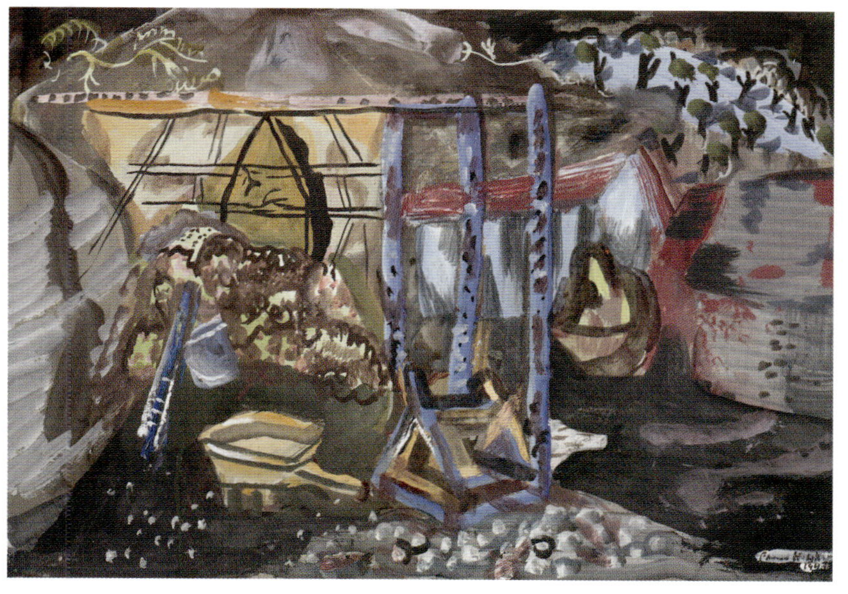

29. *The Root Crop*, 1943, gouache

status as an internationally acclaimed figure was also recognised back in New Zealand:

An artist of whom we all ought to be proud is Miss Frances Hodgkins, who now takes her place among the best in England ... doing work that is original, not a servile copy of Nature, but showing a mind of her own. She is undoubtedly the best artist we have produced, and, as far as I know, she has fought her own battle.[28]

Despite distractions such as the publication of her book, organising material for four solo exhibitions, a period of hospitalisation for a bout of illness and the tense later stages of war, Hodgkins produced a substantial amount of work. Yet, she found the need to escape from wartime dangers in coastal Corfe Castle, and so in 1942, Hodgkins returned to Wales for a few months. This time she stayed in remote Dolaucothy at an 'old Farm turned into Inn'.[29] There she created 'masses of work in between showers of torrential rain';[30] one of these paintings was most likely *The Root Crop* (Fig. 29).[31] In this work, Hodgkins punctuates the sinister landscape with complementary colours of violet, yellow and patches of magenta. The subject aligns itself with previous works such as *Quarry Farm, Wiltshire*, but in *The Root Crop*, the objects and farm are not treated with a unified spatial fluidity. Nature is now separated from its haunting ornamentation through its intense colouration.

Hodgkins, who never assumed explicit war subjects, preferred abstract references to the psychological effects she endured. There were occasions when her daily life in Corfe proved too overwhelming even to paint: 'The village is stiff with troops ... The planes overhead bringing back wounded from Normandy have scared all art out of me – I simply cannot paint.'[32] When she did gather enough strength, Hodgkins composed some of her most memorable war works, such as the apocalyptic scene, *The Courtyard in Wartime* (Fig. 30). Hodgkins' decision to paint the courtyard outside of her studio

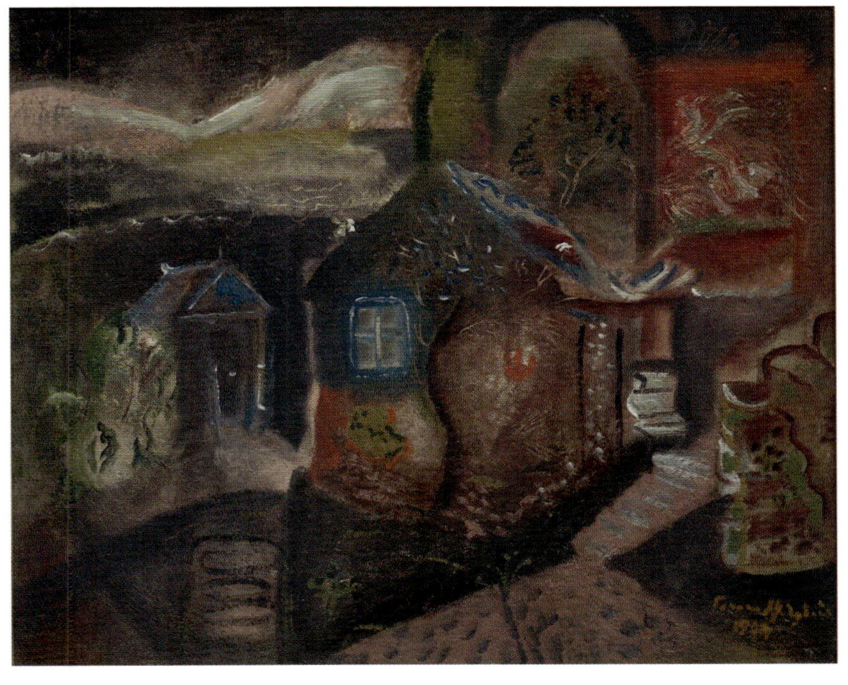

30. *The Courtyard in Wartime*, 1944, oil on board
31. (overleaf) *Spring at Little Woolgarston*, 1946, gouache on cardboard

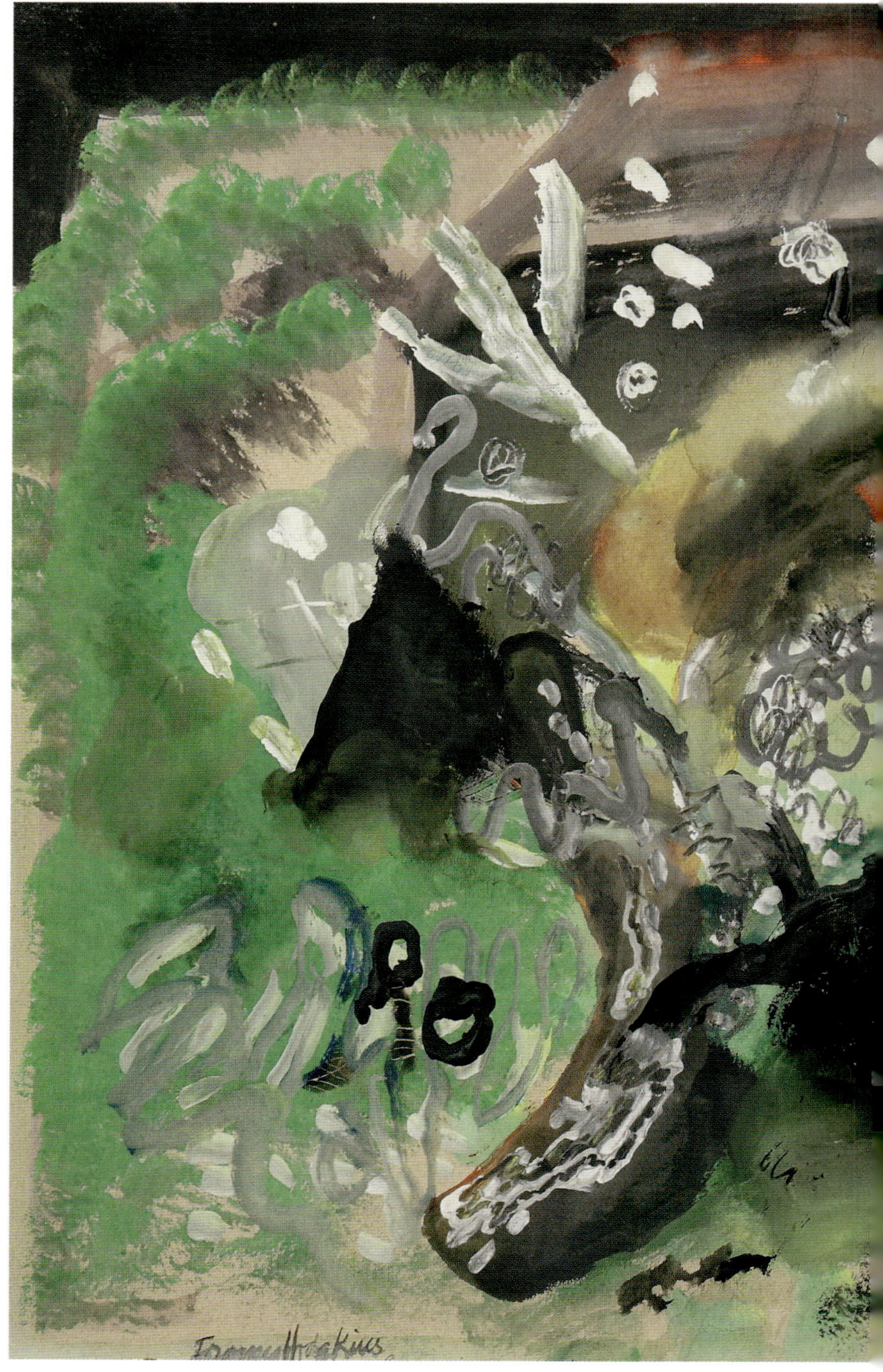

Frances Hodgkins.

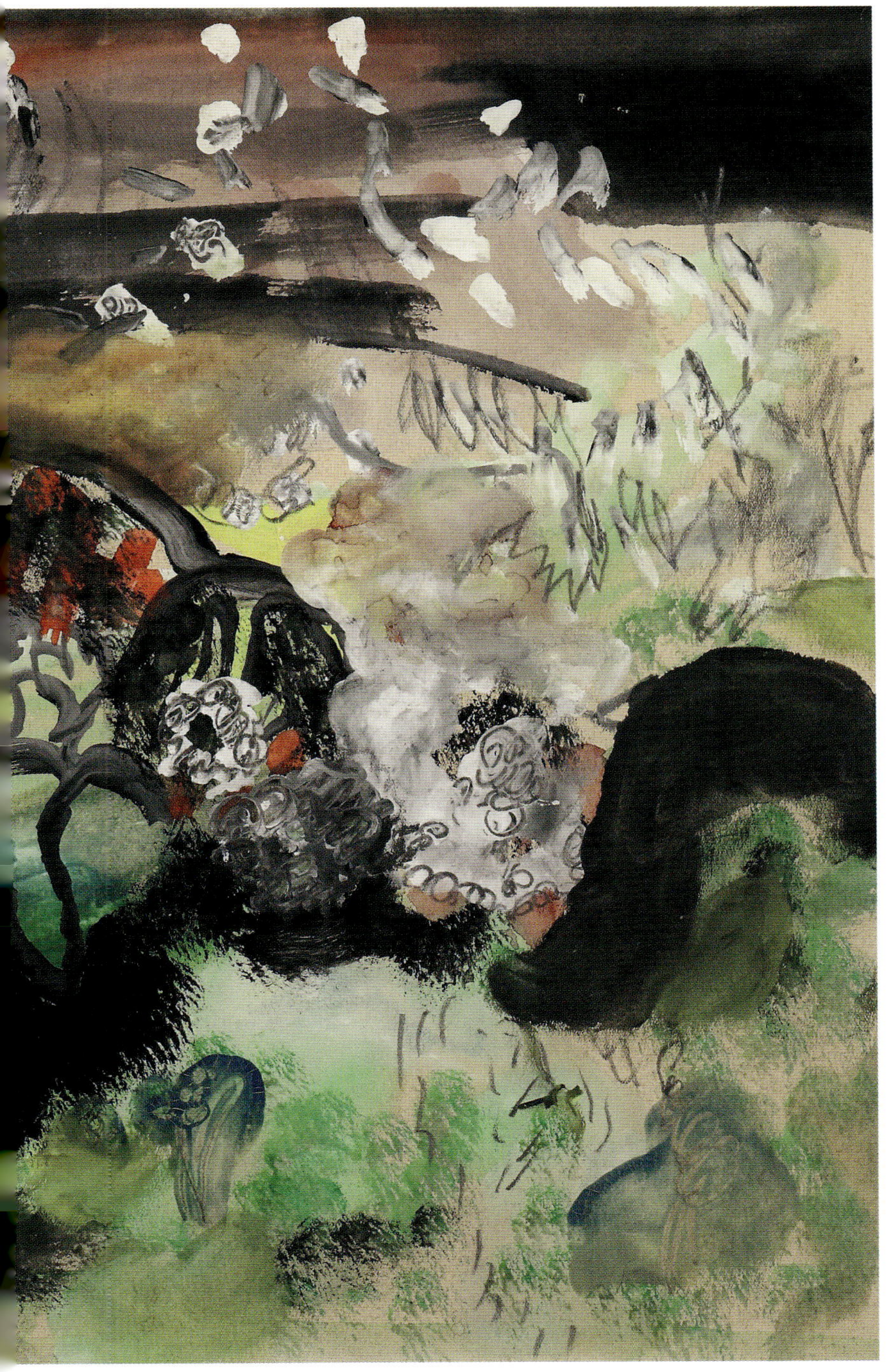

in the blackness of the night underscores her endless sense of fear during wartime. The abstracted view alongside her dramatic use of colours reinforces an emotional intensity. She also interweaves Surrealism into this Neo-Romantic painting with the mysteriously disengaged stairs, leading to an unknown destination.

After the war ended, a year before her death and at the age of 77, Hodgkins painted one of her final gouaches, *Spring at Little Woolgarston* (Fig. 31). Although the colour black lingers, the radiant green, as well as the staccato strokes of white, generate an optimistic feeling of rebirth and renewal. In November, Hodgkins reached the peak of her career when she was honoured with a retrospective exhibition of her work, dating from 1902 to 1946, at the Lefevre Galleries in London. Not long after, she contracted an illness and passed away in a psychiatric hospital near Dorchester.

Hodgkins' Reign

I feel that if I had known what was before me, I should never have had the courage to begin.[33]

The path to success for Frances Hodgkins was no small feat. She began her career as a colonial Impressionist, yet achieved an international reputation and earned an equal position amongst the most significant British modern artists by the end of her life. Her art conveyed not just a typical Modernist interest in abstraction, but also highlighted the interconnection between decoration and Modernism, by incorporating a unique artistic perspective shaped by her life experiences as a woman. Hodgkins' 'feminine' mode of Modernism, that is her unification of inner spontaneous sensations with abstracted decorative arrangements, attests to the importance of women's art at this time. Her entirely individual practice contributed to major liberations and, consequently, developments within the British

Modernist context. What is particularly revolutionary about Hodgkins' work, in relation to other Modernists, is her negotiation between her identity as a woman and the form her art assumed, as it continues to subvert the alleged inferiority of the 'typically female' in art to this day. Hodgkins' salient self-understanding enabled her to work in a dissimilar way to the aesthetic practices of most female Modernists in twentieth-century Britain, since she never resisted decorative imagery and employed a romantic yet fearless palette, so often characterised as essentially 'feminine'. Hodgkins, after all, embraced the fact that she was a 'modern woman artist'.

Notes

1 Frances Hodgkins quoted by AG Stephens, 'Frances Hodgkins: A Dunedin Girl who Conquered Paris', *Otago Daily Times*, 3 May 1913, p.5.

2 Frances Hodgkins to Isabel Field, 26 Jun 1895, in Linda Gill (ed.), *Letters of Frances Hodgkins* (Auckland 1993), p.37.

3 Frances Hodgkins to Rachel Hodgkins, 26 Aug 1901, Gill (cited note 2), p.97.

4 Frances Hodgkins to Dorothy Richmond, 7 Mar 1903, ibid., p.156.

5 Stephens (cited note 1), p.5.

6 AG Stephens, 'Frances Hodgkins', Supplement to *The Bookfellow*, Sydney, 1 May 1913, pp.ix–x.

7 For instance, in 1910, Hodgkins exhibited at the Galerie Georges Petit with the *Société Internationale d'Aquarellistes*, and a critic, who reviewed the annual exhibition, wrote: 'for one is not accustomed to expect so many good things in the lighter medium . . . Perhaps the most daring in originality, are the works of Frances Hodgkins . . .', 'Paris Letter', *American Art News*, Oct 1910. In 1911, Hodgkins exhibited with Paris's *Société de la Peinture à l'Eau*.

8 Frances Hodgkins to Rachel Hodgkins, 17 Feb 1915, Gill (cited note 2), p.303.

9 John Salis, *New Witness*, 24 Feb 1916. National Library Information File, V&A in Press Cuttings International Society's exhibitions at the Grosvenor Gallery.

10 Frances Hodgkins to John Rothenstein, 7 Oct 1945, Gill (cited note 2), p.563.

11 Sutherland stated: 'she [Hodgkins] was virtually the only one who was artistically emancipated and was already speaking the language which gradually spelt freedom in art.' June Opie, 'The Quest for Frances Hodgkins', *Ascent* 1, no. 5, Dec 1969, p.61. Piper, who collected Hodgkins' works, also found her free experimentation to be an inspiring influence, see, for instance, Anthony West, *John Piper* (London 1979), pp.87–8.

12 Frances Hodgkins to Isabel Field, 29 Aug 1925, Gill (cited note 2), p.391.

13 In a recording of Arthur Lett-Haines, a fellow artist and friend of Hodgkins, he commented on this region's influence on her art. BBC Documentary of Frances Hodgkins 1969, Tate Archives, TGA 8317.6.4.11.

14 Frances Hodgkins to Isabel Field, 3 Dec 1926, Gill (cited note 2), p.396.

15 Frances Hodgkins to Arthur Howell, 23 Sep 1930, ibid., p.434.

16 Recording transcript of Cedric Morris for the BBC Documentary of Frances Hodgkins 1969, Tate Archives, TGA 8317.6.4.12.

17 Frances Hodgkins to Lucy Wertheim, c.24 Feb 1930, Gill (cited note 2), p.424.

18 Now past her midlife, Hodgkins feared critics would stop considering her work seriously, or that the public would be biased against buying art from an older artist. More on this in the recording transcript of Cedric Morris for the BBC Documentary of Frances Hodgkins 1969, Tate Archives, TGA 8317.6.4.12.

19 Myfanwy Evans, 'Frances Hodgkins – An Appreciation of a Great Painter and Great Personality', *Vogue,* Aug 1947, pp.53, 91.

20 In 'Modernity and the spaces of femininity', Griselda Pollock explores the domestic sphere as a socially acceptable environment for women to exist in. Unlike Nicholson, Hodgkins breaks free from patriarchal bourgeois constraints by placing her still lifes outside in the open landscape. See Griselda Pollock, 'Modernity and the spaces of femininity', *Vision and Difference: Femininity, Feminism and Histories of Art* (London and New York 1988), pp.70–127.

21 Upon reviewing one of her exhibitions in 1936, Bell wrote: 'Here is essentially feminine painting; gay, intelligent and never pushed beyond her scope ... Miss Hodgkins' pictures make us think of those comments on life with which some women often charm us, the least bit artificial ... maybe, influenced possibly by a man, but illuminating.' Object label D.1939.17, Frances Hodgkins, *Still life*, drawing, 1939, The University of Manchester, The Whitworth. For further discussion of this topic, see Griselda Pollock and Rozsiker Parker (eds), *Old Mistresses: Women, Art and Ideology* (London 1981), pp.37–49.

22 EH McCormick, *Portrait of Frances Hodgkins* (Auckland 1981), p.5.

23 John Piper, 'Frances Hodgkins', *Horizon* 4, no. 24, Dec 1941, p.413.

24 Frances Hodgkins to Duncan Macdonald, c.12 Nov 1936, Gill (cited note 2), pp.471–2.

25 John Piper, *British Romantic Artists* (London 1942), p.47.

26 Frances Hodgkins to Myfanwy Evans, Mar 1943, Gill (cited note 2), p.533.

27 Frances Hodgkins to Myfanwy Evans, 12 Jun 1945, ibid., p.539.

28 AH O'Keeffe, 'Art in Retrospect', *Art in New Zealand,* Mar 1940.

29 Frances Hodgkins to Dorothy Selby, c.16 Sep 1942, Gill (cited note 2), p.528.

30 Frances Hodgkins to Eardley Knollys, 31 Oct 1942, ibid., p.530.

31 Although this work is dated 1943, the artist was known to have started a painting and then returned to it at a later date, which was probably the case for this gouache.

32 Frances Hodgkins to Dorothy Selby, 26 Jun 1944, Gill (cited note 2), p.551.

33 Stephens (cited note 6), pp.ix–x.

Image credits

1. Frances Hodgkins at her studio in Corfe Castle village, Dorset, 1945, Ref: 35mm- 00335-A-F, Alexander Turnbull Library, Wellington, New Zealand.
2. *Calves for Sale, Les Andelys, Normandy*, 1901, watercolour, 20 × 15.5 cm, Jonathan Grant Galleries, Auckland, New Zealand (www.franceshodgkins.com).
3. *The Orange Sellers, Tangier*, 1903, watercolour, 37.5 × 50 cm, Olveston Historic Home, Dunedin, New Zealand.
4. *At the Window*, c.1912, watercolour, 65.3 × 62.8 cm, South Australian Government Grant 1913, Art Gallery of South Australia, Adelaide, 0.405.
5. *Loveday and Ann: Two Women with a Basket of Flowers*, 1915, oil on canvas, 67.3 × 67.3 cm, © Tate, London 2019.
6. *Cassis*, c.1920–30, chalk, 33.7 × 38.2 cm, Auckland Art Gallery Toi o Tāmaki, purchased 1972.
7. *Untitled (Textile design, no. I)*, c.1925, gouache on paper, 41.8 × 50.0 cm, Museum of New Zealand Te Papa Tongarewa, purchased 1998 with New Zealand Lottery Grants Board Funds.
8. *Untitled (Textile design, no. IV)*, c.1925, gouache on paper, 29.2 × 20.7 cm, Museum of New Zealand Te Papa Tongarewa, purchased 1998 with New Zealand Lottery Grants Board funds.
9. *Printed Textile (Block print on silk handkerchief)*, c.1926, block print on silk, 25.3 × 27.5 cm, collection of the Dunedin Public Art Gallery.
10. *Still Life*, 1929, oil on canvas, 73 × 60 cm, The Fletcher Trust Collection.
11. *Still Life: Eggs, Tomatoes and Mushrooms*, c.1929, oil on canvas, 64 × 53 cm, Royal Pavilion & Museum, Brighton & Hove.
12. *Red Jug*, 1931, oil on canvas, 68.5 × 57 cm, Auckland Art Gallery Toi o Tāmaki, purchased 1982.
13. *Still Life with Fruit Dishes*, c.1931–7, oil on canvas laid on hardboard, 64 × 52.8 cm, collection of the Dunedin Public Art Gallery.
14. *Still Life with Red Jar*, c.1933, watercolour, 46.5 × 42 cm, collection of Christchurch Art Gallery Te Puna O Waiwhetū, purchased with assistance from the National Art Collections Fund, London, 1994.

15. Cedric Morris, *Portrait of Frances Hodgkins*, 1928, oil on canvas, 73.6 × 60.3 cm, Auckland Art Gallery Toi o Tāmaki, purchased with funds from the William James Jobson Trust, 1954. © Estate of Cedric Morris/ Bridgman Images.

16. *Portrait of Cedric Morris (Man with Macaw)*, 1930, oil on canvas, 65 × 54 cm Image Towner Art Gallery, Eastbourne.

17. *Wings over Water*, 1930, oil on canvas, 71.1 × 91.4 cm, © Tate, London 2019.

18. *The Lake (or River Garden Bridgnorth)*, c.1930–5, gouache on paper, 43.2 × 54.6 cm, © Tate, London 2019.

19. *Pleasure Garden*, 1932, watercolour, 87.5 × 75 cm, collection of Christchurch Art Gallery Te Puna O Waiwhetū, presented by a group of subscribers, 1951.

20. *Spring in the Ravine*, c.1933, oil on canvas, 62.6 × 76.1 cm, Gift of the Massey Collection of English Painting, 1946, National Gallery of Canada, Ottawa, Photo: NGC.

21. *Road to the hills, Ibiza*, 1933, watercolour, 41.4 × 55.5 cm, Museum of New Zealand Te Papa Tongarewa, purchased 1975.

22. *Still Life: Self-Portrait*, c.1935, oil on panel, 97.5 × 62.5 cm, Museum of New Zealand Te Papa Tongarewa, purchased 1999 with New Zealand Lottery Grants Board funds.

23. *Self Portrait: Still Life*, c.1935, oil on cardboard, 76.2 × 63.5 cm, Auckland Art Gallery Toi o Tāmaki, purchased 1963.

24. *Pumpkins and Pimenti*, c.1935–6, gouache, pencil and chalk, 51 × 71 cm, The Fletcher Trust Collection.

25. *Quarry Farm, Wiltshire*, c.1937, oil on canvas, 74.9 × 100.4 cm, Museum of New Zealand Te Papa Tongarewa, purchased 1975.

26. *Study for Pembrokeshire Landscape*, 1938, gouache, 52.7 × 77.5 cm, Auckland Art Gallery Toi o Tāmaki, purchased 1956.

27. *Courtyard, Corfe Castle*, 1942, gouache, ink and charcoal, 49.7 × 61.7 cm, Art Gallery of New South Wales, gift of the Contemporary Art Society, London 1944, Photo: Diana Panuccio, AGNSW, 7434.

28. *Broken Tractor*, 1942, gouache on paper, 38.1 × 57.1 cm, © Tate, London 2019.

29. *The Root Crop*, 1943, gouache, 38.2 x 56.6 cm, Auckland Art Gallery Toi o Tāmaki, purchased with funds from the Winstone Bequest, 1954.

30. *The Courtyard in Wartime*, 1944, oil on board, 61 × 76.2 cm, University of Auckland Art Collection.

31. *Spring at Little Woolgarston*, 1946, gouache on cardboard, 36.4 × 50 cm, Museum of New Zealand Te Papa Tongarewa, bequest of Judge Julius Isaacs, New York, 1983.

About the author

Samantha Niederman is a PhD candidate at the University of York, and her research examines the Romantic Modernist pictorial language of Frances Hodgkins and Cedric Morris. Before commencing her thesis, Samantha served as Curatorial Assistant at the Norton Museum of Art, where she contributed research and assisted with the organisation of *O'Keeffe, Stettheimer, Torr, Zorach: Women Modernists in New York*. She received an MA from University College of London, an MLitt from the University of Glasgow and a BA in the History of Art & Architecture from Boston University.

Acknowledgements

This book would not have been possible without the generosity and support from a number of colleagues, curators and institutions. I am indebted to Katy Norris, my friend and fellow PhD student, who first brought this project to my attention and recommended my contribution on Frances. I would also like to thank a number of curators and institutions for generously agreeing to waive their fees in support of this project: Mary Kisler, Senior Curator, Auckland Art Gallery Toi o Tāmaki; Peter Shaw, Curator, The Fletcher Trust Collection; Jonathan Gooderham, Director, Jonathan Grant Galleries Ltd; Bronwyn Simes, Manager, Olveston Historic Home; Royal Pavilion & Museum, Brighton & Hove; Karen Taylor, Collections Curator, Towner Art Gallery; Sam Melser, Collection Assistant, University of Auckland Art Collection.

Finally, I am particularly grateful to Harriet Judd, Founder of Eiderdown Books, who not only offered me the invaluable opportunity to contribute to this Modern Women Artists series, but she also inspired and motivated many of us women with her courageous endeavour to start her own all-female publishing company.

Index

Page numbers in *italic* refer to the illustrations

A

Académie Colarossi, Paris 1
Art Deco 14
Art Nouveau 14

B

Balearic Islands 28
Bell, Clive, *Art* 11
Biennale di Venezia (1940) 41
Blake, William 34
Bodinnick, Cornwall 23
Bonnard, Pierre 8

C

Calico Printers' Association (CPA)
    14–15
Cassis *10*, 11
Cézanne, Paul 11, 18
Clark, Sir Kenneth 41
Claude Lorrain 2
colonial Impressionism 1, 2– 4, 23, 48
Constructivism 29
Corfe Castle, Dorset 37, *40*, 44
Cubism 15, 18

D

Dunedin, New Zealand 1

E

Evans, Myfanwy 23, 41
*Exposition Internationale des Arts
    Décoratifs*, Paris (1925) 14

F

Fauvism 4
First World War 5–8
France 5–8, 11, 23
Fry, Roger
    Vision and Design 14

H

Hepworth, Barbara 29
Hitchens, Ivon 29
Hodgkins, Frances *Frontispiece, 24*
    achieves recognition 41–4
    death 48
    exhibitions 5, 8, 15, 41, 44, 48
    financial problems 14, 22
    framing technique 18, 23
    friendship with Cedric Morris 22–3
    health problems 44
    interest in ruins 37–41
    and Modernism 2–5, 29, 41, 48–9
    as a Neo-Romantic Modernist
        34–48
    'open-air still lifes' 15–18
    in Second World War 23, 37, 44–8
    self-portraits 29
    still lifes 4, 34
    teaching career 1, 5–8
    textile designs 14–15, 18

Hodgkins, Frances (cont.)
  use of colour 4, 28, 29
  watercolours 4, 5–8, 11
  At the Window 5, 7, 23–8
  Broken Tractor 37–41, *42*
  *Calves for Sale, Les Andelys,
    Normandy* 2–4, *3*
  Cassis 10, 11
  Cedric Morris (Man with Macaw)
    22–3, *25*
  Courtyard, Corfe Castle 37, 40,
    41
  The Courtyard in Wartime 44–8,
    45
  *The Lake (or River Garden
    Bridgnorth)* 27, 28
  Loveday and Ann 8–11, *9*, 28
  The Orange Sellers, Tangier 4, 6,
    34
  Pleasure Garden 28, *30*
  *Printed Textile (Block print on silk
    handkerchief)* 13, 15
  Pumpkins and Pimenti 34, *35*,
    37
  Quarry Farm, Wiltshire 34–7, *36*, 37,
    44
  Red Jug 18, *19*
  Road to the hills, Ibiza 28, *31*
  The Root Crop 43, 44
  Self-Portrait: Still Life 29, *33*
  Spring at Little Woolgarston 46–7,
    48
  Spring in the Ravine 28, *31*
  Still Life *16*, 18
  *Still Life: Eggs, Tomatoes and
    Mushrooms* *17*, 18, 22
  Still Life: Self-Portrait 29, *32*
  Still Life with Fruit Dishes 18, *20*
  Still Life with Red Jar 18, *21*
  *Study for Pembrokeshire
    Landscape* 37, *38–9*
  Untitled (Textile design, no. I) *12*,
    14
  Untitled (Textile design, no. IV) 13,
    14
  Wings over Water 23–8, *26*
Howell, Arthur R. 15

I
Ibiza, Balearic Islands 28
Impressionism 11
  colonial Impressionism 1, 2–4, 23,
    48
*International Surrealist Exhibition,
  London (1936)* 34

L
Lefevre Galleries, London 48
Lett-Haines, Arthur 22
London 4, 11, 15, 22, 23, 34, 48
London Group 15

M
McCormick, Eric Hall 29
Manchester 14
Marseilles 11
Matisse, Henri 4
Melbourne 14
Modernism 2–4, 5, 8–11, 29, 41,
  48–9
Morocco 4
Morris, Cedric 22–3, *25*
  Portrait of Frances Hodgkins 22,
    24
Moss, Marlow 29

N
Nabis 8
Nash, Paul 22
National Portrait Society, London 8
Neo-Primitivism 28
Neo-Romanticism 11, 34–48
New English Art Club 15
New Zealand 1, 2, 5
Newlyn, Cornwall 8, 22
Nicholson, Ben 29

Nicholson, Winifred 29
Normandy 2, 44

P
Palmer, Samuel 34
Paris 1, 5–8, 14
The Penguin Modern Painters
    series 1, 41
Penzance, Cornwall 8
Picasso, Pablo 15
Piper, John 22, 34, 37
    British Romantic Artists 41
Polynesian art 14
Post-Impressionism 11
Pound Farm, Higham, Suffolk 22–3
Poussin, Nicolas 2

R
Redon, Odilon 4
Romanticism 34
Royal Academy of Arts, London 4, 15

S
St George's Gallery, London 15
St Ives, Cornwall 8, 11
Second World War 23, 37, 44–8
Seven and Five Society 15, 22, 29, 37
Spain 23
Surrealism 34, 48
Sutherland, Graham 22, 41
Symbolism 4

T
Tangier, Morocco 4
Tate Gallery, London 11

V
Venice 41
Vuillard, Édouard 8

W
Wales 37, 44
Wallis, Alfred 28